Taking It Back

Life Beyond Childhood Sexual Abuse

Chuck Tyler

KATHRYN —
THANK YOU FOR YOUR
LOVE AND SUPPORT!
MISS YOU!
— CHUCK

DEDICATION

This book is dedicated to sexual abuse survivors everywhere.

The strength you have already displayed
in living through your sexual violation
is proof that you have the strength
to heal from it.
Know that whatever your experience was,
there is healing for you.
There is a life of peace for you.
Be honest with yourself.
Be present and aware.
Know that nobody can keep you
from shedding the weight of past events,
from taking back your power
and from becoming the peaceful, loving self
that you know you are.

CONTENTS

THANK YOU

To my wife, Alissa, who's years of continuous love and support have made it possible for me to not only share my story in this book, but to also find an empowered life with someone who truly loves me for who I am.

To my brother, Jim, for his loving, nonjudgmental support from the very beginning of my recovery journey to this very day.

To Jim Blush, for being one of the two adult males in my life who allowed me to maintain trust in an adult man when I was a child.

To Donna Dershem, for offering her caring support as the first person I turned to in those early days of my journey.

And to my dog, Levi, for being my rock in those early days when I was alone and trying to figure everything out.

INTRODUCTION

It seems that every abuse survivor I speak with has a different story to tell me about their abuse. Age, location, frequency, duration, family members, non-family members, one abuser, multiple abusers... I think it's important to take a moment and understand that there is no one single scenario, story or situation that can definitively describe what people call sexual abuse, sexual trauma or sexual violation. Additionally, your story is no more or less valid than anyone else's story. If you personally were abused one time and somebody else endured ten years of abuse, it in no way invalidates the physical, emotional or psychological pain you endured or are still experiencing. Don't compare your experience with anyone else's situation in an effort to define whether or not you were "abused". If you have been hurt by something that someone else did to you, if trust has been broken, then what you're feeling is valid. It's up to you to decide whether or not you want to learn how to heal from it, to learn how to let go of what happened and to move forward with a life of freedom from what someone else did to you.

It wasn't until decades after my sexual abuse ended that I finally realized I was living in the heavy emotional aftermath of it. I decided intentionally to do something about it. I had no roadmap through the recovery process. I was at such a low emotional point in my life that I just needed to get off of that island of despair. So I dove into the ocean and started swimming. I decided that any direction would do. I just needed to get somewhere else.

In retrospect, I blazed a trail through uncharted territory, not knowing where it would lead or how long it would take. My journey eventually led me away from depression, self-blame, hate, anger and confusion. I finally found peace and forgiveness, which are things I never thought I would feel after being sexually abused. When I look back at my darkest times of solitude and despair, I remember coming to the conclusion that life was simply pain and that I just needed to accept that. It wasn't until I reached the very beginning stages of recovery that I realized how wrong I was to think that. I was just lost with no obvious path or direction to lead me away from that seemingly bottomless pit I was in. I wrote this book as a guide to help people who are in that very situation.

As I speak to audiences, and also to individual people, about my techniques of healing from the wounds of sexual abuse, people inevitably ask me about the intimate details of my personal story. At first I thought this was just curiosity, but I've come to realize that people who have been sexually abused, and also loved ones of people in recovery, can connect with hearing the details of my personal story in a helpful way. Hearing and digesting the details of my abuse situation helps them put together the pieces of their own lives in a deeper and more intimate way than simply hearing my healing methodologies.

With that in mind, I wrote this book differently than a typical self-help book. I wanted to not only share my advice and experience about healing from sexual abuse, but I also wanted to share my personal story of abuse in detail to illicit that deeper, emotional connection which can only come from that kind of sharing. So, along with my advice for those recovering from sexual abuse, this book is also a chronological recounting of my experiences as an abused child, my struggles as an adolescent and young man, my challenges as an adult and finally my awakening and focused recovery as a middle-aged man. Hopefully the details I share of my abuse mixed with the wisdom I've achieved in recovery will give you, the reader, a more expansive and valuable understanding of how to move forward with your own situation.

At the beginning of my journey, when I was ready to start digging for the source of the pain I was feeling, it became immediately clear that I had to be honest with myself - to be exposed and vulnerable about everything, otherwise it would all just be a waste of time. As I started unpacking all the experiences and emotions from my youth that had built up and were weighing on me as an adult, I was amazed at how much there was. It seemed like the more I dug, the more I found. I very quickly discovered that it wasn't just the incidents of sexual abuse that affected me, but also the environment that surrounded me during that abusive time. Abuse doesn't happen in a vacuum. There is always an environment surrounding the abuse that, in whatever way, allowed it to happen. There were elements from these surroundings that added to the side effects of my abuse, and it was awareness and examination of them which greatly helped in my recovery.

Lastly, let me say from personal experience that, no matter how disempowered or helpless you may feel, how angry, hateful or depressed you may be, we all have the strength in us to embark on that intentional journey of recovery. Whatever your experience with sexual violation was, know that there is healing and a life of peace for you. My hope is that this book will bring you comfort, direction and hope for your journey.

CHUCK TYLER

CHAPTER 1

WAS I REALLY ABUSED?

"There are wounds that never show on the body,
that are deeper and more hurtful
than anything that bleeds."

- Laurell K. Hamilton

WHAT MAKES ME THINK I WAS ABUSED?

This is a common question that I was asked by people who were not quick to believe me when I shared my story with them. Ultimately, these people were either my friends or family; people who already knew me but had never heard me talk about being abused before. To answer these people, I told them that I had repressed memories of the abuse that were finally resurfacing. This was the easiest way to explain it to them, but the truth was more complicated than that.

"Abuse" is a pretty vague term. I have found, through talking to people, that the definition of abuse can change or become grey when it comes to how parents raise their children. Not only do parents have varying methodologies for raising their children, they have different definitions of what constitutes acceptable disciplinary action. I always thought I came from a pretty average family. I was the youngest of four children in my family. My oldest brother and sister were almost a decade older than me, and my other brother was just two years older than me. He and I essentially grew up together, while my two older siblings were off doing their own things with people their own age.

I was an intelligent, creative child and I had a lot of energy. I was labeled a troublemaker when I was in grade school and middle school, and I always attributed it to feeling bored in class. I went to grade school in rural Oklahoma, in the mid to late 1970's. Back in those days, when kids misbehaved in class, it was standard procedure in my public school for the teacher to walk us down to the principal's office, make us bend over his desk, and then hit us several times with a wooden paddle. These teachers weren't joking around either, they would hit us hard. Depending on the teacher, this punishment sometimes took place in front of the classroom at the teacher's desk, so that everyone in the class could watch the physical abuse and emotional humiliation. In retrospect, I consider this to be child abuse. At the time, these classroom beatings were an unquestioned part of my public school environment; it was simply the way things were done. Teachers, students and even parents accepted it as standard school policy.

Up until that point in my life, I had lived in bigger cities like Houston, Pittsburg and Toronto. In these bigger city schools, even back in the 1970's, teachers didn't hit children in class. But when our family moved to rural Oklahoma, I realized that public school policy, as well as the overall energy of the school, seemed to be decades older. Coming from my previous nonviolent classroom environment, into a situation where violence was commonplace, felt inherently wrong to me. However, the students who had grown up in this small Oklahoma town, were raised to accept that being beaten and humiliated in school was simply a part of life. Some of my classmates would also talk casually about how they were beaten at home by their parents, spanked, or even hit with a belt, for doing something wrong.

Surrounded by these physically and emotionally violent standards, I never thought about using the word "abuse" to define anything that was going on in my home. My parents never hit me or spanked me like my friends told me about. They punished me in other ways like refusing to let me watch TV or sending me to my room instead of being allowed to play with other kids in the neighborhood after school. My parents argued a lot throughout my childhood and eventually divorced when I was in my early teens. After a couple of stressful years living alone with my mother, I left home at seventeen and started out on my adult life journey without ever thinking I was sexually abused.

My memories of sexual abuse started surfacing in my late twenties. Some abuse survivors I've talked with in recent years told me that they had sudden, vivid and shocking memories resurface of their abuse, sometimes while in public or while having conversations with other people. My experience of surfacing memories was not as sudden. For me, the memories started gradually sneaking into my conscious mind in pieces, mostly as vague or nonspecific homosexual thoughts. I was in the middle of getting my art degree when it began, so I attributed these strange thoughts to that environment of exercising bold creativity in my thinking. I had always been heterosexual, so when these memories began to surface over the course of several years, I dealt with them by not taking them seriously and by ultimately ignoring them.

When I finally did admit to myself that these resurfacing memories had been prominently appearing in my mind for a couple of years, the realization was quite a shock. It was as much of a shock to realize that I had been ignoring such disturbing memories for so long. This realization happened one day when I was thirty years old, while I was cleaning out the basement of my house. (I suppose I could attach some symbolism to that.) When I suddenly admitted to myself that I had been having ongoing homosexual thoughts that would not subside, my only logical conclusion was that I must be gay, and I must only just now be admitting it to myself. As if this wasn't enough of a kick to the head, I simultaneously had the realization that my father may have sexually abused me as a child. (In retrospect, it's hard to believe both realizations happened at the same time.) This was all mixed together in a big confusing and shocking mess in my head. It was as if I opened a door to an old closet and all this stuff came tumbling out. I felt like I suddenly didn't know who I was and was faced with a massive identity crisis.

I started sorting through the specific memories that made me think I was abused. Some of the memories were intimate images of my father that I felt like the average person really should not have. I had images of parts of his body, being in his bedroom on his bed and us being naked together – sometimes in the shower. I remembered always feeling extremely uncomfortable throughout my childhood whenever he would put his hands on me, in public or in private. I remember his physical touch was nauseating. In the early stages of sorting through these memories, one very vivid memory I had, was when he walked right into the bathroom while I was showering, looked over the shower door and his eyes went right down to my crotch. This was one memory that was not suppressed and which always bothered me. But were these memories enough to build a case for sexual abuse? At the time, it seemed like such a leap from having a few weird memories to making such a disgusting accusation. I came to learn later how it was just that kind of self-doubt which allowed me to tell myself it never happened, and to help keep those memories suppressed for so many years.

I think there are environmental factors which helped my memories of sexual abuse surface when they did. First of all, when the memories started to surface, I was in the first really supportive romantic relationship of my life. This made me feel safe and protected. Secondly, I was living in a very isolated location, in the foothills of the Rocky Mountains. The nearest gas station or convenience store was a fifteen minute drive. Third, where I was living, I didn't have the distractions of cable TV or internet, so I spent my personal time either reading, hiking in the mountains or thinking. I believe another reason these memories came back during this time in my life is because, I believe the human body *wants* to heal itself and my brain believed I was strong enough to deal with these terrible memories. (I discuss suppressed memories more in Chapter 4.)

Out of confusion and curiosity, I was eventually brave enough to make an appointment with a therapist a few months after my basement experience. This was my first experience with one-on-one therapy. And it was important to me to talk with someone who specialized in abuse. On my first visit, the therapist asked me to talk about every memory I could think of regarding my father, as he made notes. After about half an hour of note-taking, he stopped me and showed me a list of specific memories that he had written down as I talked. He had organized a couple dozen of my memories that my mind clearly wasn't allowing me to put together on my own. As I looked at his list of neatly assembled memories, it was painfully obvious that I had definitely been sexually abused by my father. This therapist had connected the dots for me and allowed me to see my situation from an outside perspective. After getting over the shock of this realization, this knowledge was a starting point for me; a trailhead.

Over the next several months, and actually years, as I settled into the realization that I had been abused, my mind allowed more memories to slowly surface and the big picture of my abusive childhood started to take shape.

If you are experiencing resurfacing memories, or you "think" you're having memories, my advice is to follow up with them. These thoughts, memories, or feelings inside of you are coming to the surface for a reason. If you notice that you've been ignoring them for a certain period of time, possibly years, then ask yourself WHY you have been ignoring them. It's possible that your mind has been trying to keep you from experiencing painful, frightening memories for a period of time, and now is letting them resurface. My advice is to shine a light on whatever memories are trying to get your attention. Be present, be aware and most of all, be honest with yourself. This is the beginning of a healing journey for you. This is your opportunity to choose to take it! Get to the bottom of what you're experiencing. Get to the truth.

WHAT IS SEXUAL ABUSE?

The legal definition of sexual abuse varies in different states or countries and usually includes the word "child" or "minor", but not always. When it does include the word "child", it also includes the word "adult". I've also seen the words "parent", "guardian" and "relative" being used with a high frequency which is one of the indicators that the majority of sexual abuse cases are not only between adults and minors, but also between family members. The American Psychological Association defines sexual abuse as:

"Unwanted sexual activity, with perpetrators using force, making threats or taking advantage of victims not able to give consent."

Abusers are people who not only have some kind of power over another person, but who also leverage that power against their victims in a way that is unfair. In most criminal rapes, that power is physical. In the workplace, that power is usually some kind of managerial hierarchy. In my case, with my abuser being my father, it was a combination of physical, social and psychological power. He was physically bigger than me and he was the head of the household who created the rules by which we all lived while under his roof. Also, because I was so young, he also had the power of intellect over me which allowed him to plan and execute his abuse in a deceptive and manipulative way.

My opinion is that if you find yourself in a situation with a person who has some kind of power over you, and that situation makes you sexually uncomfortable, then you should get out of that situation. If that person uses their power over you to keep you in that situation, then that is sexual abuse. In other words, if you honestly FEEL like you were sexually abused, then you were. Sexual abuse does not have to involve penetration, physical force, pain, or even touching. If an adult engages in any sexual behavior (looking, showing, saying things and/or touching) with a child, or with a non-consenting adult, to meet his or her own sexual needs or interests, then that behavior is sexual abuse.

Sexual interaction between children can be considered

sexual abuse as well. The law seems to require a significant age difference of typically three or more years between the abuser and the abused. My personal feeling is that age does not matter. For one person to be in power over another person, they do not have to be older.

The word "pedophilia" is used to refer to an adult's strong and persistent sexual attraction to prepubescent children or those in the early stages of puberty. These children are typically younger than eleven years old. "Hebephelia" is term used to describe an adult attraction to children who have begun puberty, generally ages 11-14. Also, the term "ephebophilia" refers to the attraction of an adult to someone past puberty but not yet a legally consenting adult; usually 15-18 years old. Adults performing sexual acts with anyone under the age of legal sexual consent in their state or country are breaking the law by committing statutory rape. The age of consent, however, varies greatly in different parts of the world.

I researched an enormous amount of statistical information over the years, but I don't share a lot of it in this book because it's so easily acquired with an instantaneous internet search. I think these minimum ages of sexual consent that I'm about to share, however, help to illustrate the varying perspectives and perhaps definitions of legal rights between adults and children around the world. The legal age of sexual consent in the United States is 16, 17 or 18 years old, depending on which state you are in. Currently, Bahrain has the highest age of consent in the world at 21 years old, followed by South Korea at 20. Nigeria sets their age of legal sexual consent at 11 years old, which is almost the lowest in the world. I say "almost" because there are 13 countries in Asia and Africa that have no age of legal consent, but sex is not legally allowed outside of marriage. When I came across these ages in my research, I have to admit that some of them were shocking to me. But I have not been to these countries and have no first-hand knowledge of their cultures. I can only speak from my American perspective. I only know the western culture that I was raised in and the rights I was afforded. I do know, however, how little I felt I knew about making decisions in my own, best, long-term interests when I was so very young.

I have spoken to, and officially interviewed online, adults who are sexually attracted to minors of different ages. Pedophiles, hebephiles and ephebophiles have what seems to be an uncontrollable and unchangeable sexual attraction to their respective age groups. Medical science is finally starting to refer to these disorders as "orientations", like heterosexuality or homosexuality. This has sparked bitter, hateful, polarized debates about what rights pedophiles should or should not have. Regardless of what side of this debate you choose, it is important to note here that people from any of these sexually deviant groups have not broken any laws until they have acted on their desires. They are not classified as criminals until they choose to become child molesters or users of child pornography. Until that point, they are members of an overtly stigmatized group of people who will remain in hiding until the smoke of this heated, ongoing argument clears.

There are adults who sexually abuse children who are pedophiles, and there are adults who sexually abuse children who are NOT pedophiles. In fact, statistics show that the majority of child sexual abuse is perpetrated by adults who are NOT sexually attracted to children. My biggest point here is that this is a very complex issue and as a childhood sexual abuse survivor, I am right in the middle of it. My overall perspective is that we, as a society, should be focused on prevention of abuse, instead of angry, hateful reaction to it.

Regarding the gender of pedophiles, there are no exact numbers, but most pedophiles seem to be men. Even though females who sexually abuse children seem to be rare compared to the number of male pedophiles, I knew a woman who was sexually abused as a child for years by a female adult babysitter/friend of her parents. This female pedophile used all the same manipulative tactics that are common in male pedophiles, including psychological manipulation and threats.

When I tried to remember exactly what happened between my father and I, when I was so young, I didn't remember him exerting any violent, physical force over me. But, being that my memories during this time in my life were suppressed, this didn't dissuade me from digging deeper to find out more. I was sure that the strange things that I WAS remembering were making me very uncomfortable and those memories were enough for me to do some more exploration.

Regardless of any technical or legal definition, I think if someone else makes you feel uncomfortable in any situation by something they're doing, then that behavior on their part constitutes some form of abuse. It may be verbal, non verbal, or physical. When I say physical, that could mean them making physical contact with you or not making contact with you. The rock bottom truth is, if that person cares so little about your comfort in the situation, then they are willfully abusing you in some way.

An abuser can take advantage of any position of power, even if it's momentary power or perceived power. Once, when I was working at an art gallery, I had a customer (an older man) start to put his hands on me while we were talking about a painting. We were alone in the gallery. He actually started rubbing my shoulder and arm with his hand while staring into my eyes and smiling. This was absolutely abuse, if not sexual assault. Socially speaking, he thought he was in a position of power over me because I was an employee and I had to be polite to all the customers. He took advantage of his position of being the customer to leverage his perceived power against me. This happened at a point in my life when I had already done the work to fully define what abuse looked like and felt like. I ultimately was not polite to this man at all. When I told him to get his hands off me, I took his perceived power away. He removed his hands and he left the gallery.

If you have questions about the definitions of abuse, or about legal recourses, I suggest you speak with an attorney in your area or research your local laws. A wonderful resource for this is RAINN.org.

WHO WAS MY ABUSER?

The man who sexually abused me was my father. The abuse began when I was only three years old and lasted for nine years until I was eleven years old. The trauma from those years of abuse caused my brain to repress all the memories of what happened to me, so I went through my entire childhood not knowing that I was abused at all.

Research tells me that my father probably stopped abusing me when I was eleven because I became too old for his sexual preference. He apparently was not sexually attracted to me anymore, so he stopped abusing me. Instead, he took his desires in a different direction. At that time, he was not only seeing another woman behind my mother's back, but he was also very intentionally having children with her. My father and this woman had a boy and a girl together while he was still married to my mother. When I was fourteen years old, my father moved out of our home and my parents quickly divorced. Looking back, it's obvious to me now what he was doing. He already had practice sexually abusing his own child without anyone noticing, so he simply took that skill set into a new family and created younger children to abuse.

Throughout my childhood, even after the sexual abuse had ended, I had no memories of the abuse. I do, however, remember feeling continually uncomfortable around my father. For example, our family would be in the living room watching TV together and he would choose to sit on the couch next to me. Any physical contact he had with me - a hand on my leg or putting his arm around me - would give me immediate anxiety.

Later, when I was in my twenties, I still had no memory of my childhood abuse. My father lived in another state and when he would come to visit, I didn't want him touching me. During one visit, we got into several arguments over different things. When he was leaving to fly home, he came in close to give me a hug and I reflexively knocked his arms out of the way and pushed him back. I was training at a martial arts school at the time and my reflexes simply took over, knocking him a couple steps back. He was shocked and asked why I did that. I told him that I didn't want him touching me. He had no response to that comment. He just turned and walked away. This was the last time I ever saw him face-to-face. Even though all the memories of the abuse were still buried, I felt that I didn't want him being around me or having any physical contact with me, so I refused to see him anymore.

At the time, I was consciously angry at him because he left our family and divorced my mother. Unconsciously, however, I was angry at him because of the years of abuse. My family and friends never questioned my anger at him, and neither did I. The fact that he divorced my mother and left us alone when I was fourteen seemed to be enough of an excuse for me to be angry at him. That reason quelled my curiosity and I left this feeling of anger in place for years.

Through years of therapy, research and a lot of self-honesty, I realized that there were possibly one or two other men who sexually abused me during my childhood. One was a pastor at a church that my parents took me to when I was in first and second grade. This pastor also taught Sunday school classes that I attended. I have memories of his hands on me, and feeling uncomfortable.

I also remember him picking me up to hold me when it seemed inappropriate at the time. The other man who may have abused me was my public school fourth grade teacher. My memories of him included him putting his hands on the me and the other male children in class with a frequency that I thought was too often. I can not recall specific instances of sexual abuse from either of these men, but I have some very uncomfortable memories of both them being physically close to me.

It's possible that these men were pedophiles and could spot me as a target because of the submissive behavior created by the abuse I was suffering from my father. Pedophiles are adept at reading and "grooming" children (discussed more in "How Was I Abused"). Memories of being abused by these men could have been repressed along with the other memories I had of my father. Another possibility is that these men could have been pedophiles but may not have abused me at all. They may have just reminded me of my father in their predatory behavior or in some other way. Either of these would justify my uncomfortable memories of them.

Like I said before, abuse doesn't happen in a vacuum. In your own abuse situation, there were probably other people around you that your abuser had to avoid, deceive and circumnavigate to make the abuse happen. Maybe there were other people who were present did not notice what was happening. There may have also been other people around who knew about the abuse and allowed it to happen, or actively took part in the abuse. Research shows that pedophiles often work together. It's possible that you may have been abused by different people at different times in your life. (I talk about this in detail in Chapter 5.)

Thinking that I may have been abused by more than one adult when I was a child, I researched facts about pedophiles and how they work. Typically pedophiles can spot and "groom" children. Grooming is a sinister practice where pedophiles zero-in on children who exhibit certain types of behavior that would make them prone to control and manipulation. I learned that in the course of their lifetime, pedophiles could abuse as many as sixty children.

I personally don't have memories about being abused along side other children or other adults – I only have memories of my father and me. As a part of my recovery, I did recently speak to a childhood friend of mine on the phone. We are both in our fifties now. He told me that when he was visiting my family's house as a child, my father quietly exposed himself to him. My friend ignored it and said nothing. I don't know how many of my other friends my father exposed himself to, or how many of my friends he may have abused, or how many children in total he abused during his lifetime.

Current statistics show that eight out of ten children who are sexually abused know their abuser. They are typically family members, friends, neighbors or babysitters. Many abusers hold responsible positions in society like teachers, coaches and pediatricians. A friend of mine was sexually abused by his high school swim coach, giving him access to dozens of barely dressed boys. This coach was abusing several of the team members that were in his care. When they all came together and exposed him to the local press, the coach committed suicide before he could respond to the allegations. This child-abusing pedophile was in the same, small, rural Oklahoma town that my father and I were in. He also had nowhere to turn for help in dealing with his desire to sexually abuse boys. Pedophiles like he and my father have very few choices when they have nowhere to turn and typically end up as child molesters.

If you don't know who your abuser was, but you're

having memories of abuse, I recommend some form of regression therapy for possibly helping you remember. (I discuss different types of therapy in Chapter 3). If you do know who your abuser was, regression will give you a point of reference to go inward and start thinking about other memories you have of the person, or people, you feel uncomfortable about.

HOW WAS I ABUSED?

There are certainly many different kinds of sexual abuse situations. There are one-time instances of rape, molestation or exposure and there are situations of ongoing abuse or torture. Some of these are physical, some are psychological, but most are combinations. Where there is forced, physical abuse, there is absolutely psychological trauma that accompanies it. Some of the most extreme and severe cases of sexual abuse are the ones we hear about on the news, when children are kidnapped out of their home, held against their will and raped. Other children are sold into sexual slavery or forced into human trafficking. There are certainly countries in the world where torturous rape of women and children seem to be common or somehow socially accepted. The more I talk with people, especially from different parts of the world, the more variations I hear on the same stories of people who have more power taking advantage of those with less power.

My personal abuse situation was much more hidden than the "newsworthy" stories of being kidnapped and taken away. It all happened in the privacy and controlled environment of my family home. As a part of my recovery, I read stories written by adults who were kidnapped and sexually abused as children. Each story was a little different, but most of these people said that the one thing that helped them survive their kidnap and abuse was knowing that they had loving parents at home waiting for them. They told themselves that if they could just live through the abuse or escape to get back to their caring parents, everything would be alright. These cases are the minority. Most child sexual abuse situations happen within the walls of family homes and get no attention from the press.

I met a woman who's parents literally sold her into an underground pedophile cult when she was five years old, where she remained until she was in her late teens. She had no hope and no motivation of going back to her parents who sold her for money. She was completely on her own. Those of us who were abused by a parent or a guardian had no loving parental figures as motivation to escape to and no hope of the abuse ending. My situation was invisible to everyone outside of me and my abuser and it went unnoticed by the world.

When the American Medical Association called child sexual abuse "the silent epidemic", they were not referring to the high profile cases of abduction and kidnapping, they were talking about the ongoing behind-the-scenes family-based sexual abuse that effects millions of children, sending them into their adult lives with crippling side effects. The incredible trauma of being kidnapped, taken away by someone outside of your family and sexually abused is equally terrible and also very different than the trauma of being sexually abused at home by someone within your family.

If you find yourself comparing your own experience of abuse to any other story that you may have heard, please take a moment to be aware of WHY you are doing it. Comparing someone else's situation to your own, in order to judge whether or not your experience is considered "abuse", is not an accurate or productive thing do to. Some stories, especially ones promoted by the media, are so terrible that it may prompt you to think, "I didn't go through something that bad. I must not really have been abused." This kind of comparison is never fair to you. You know in your heart whether or not you were abused because you can feel it.

Hearing other people's stories of sexual abuse can be difficult, but it can also be empowering. Listening to other people tell their stories helped me to realize that I was not alone in my own experience, that sexual abuse has happened to other people who were also not at fault for what happened to them, and that others have both survived and overcome the long-term side effects of their own abuse situations. Listening to people speak the truth, that they may have been hiding inside for so long, was also an inspiration for me to speak my own truth and to tell my story. I think the more people that speak up, the better we all are.

Through years of therapy, which helped to bring back specific memories, I now know that my father was both physically and sexually abusive to me. He used me to fulfill his sexual desires without regard to the effects it had - or would have - on me, my behavior or my self worth for the rest of my life. The physical and sexual abuse was not a one-time event, it lasted for nine years. The psychological abuse went on for years after that while I still lived with him and was not being physically abused. Although these memories were suppressed for decades, my first therapy sessions brought back enough memories for me to be absolutely sure I was abused. It wasn't until years later that specific memories of exactly what he did to me surfaced. The memories would pop in at random times, while I was working around my house, at work, or with friends.

Additionally, through therapy, I learned that my parents' divorce and my father leaving, which happened in my early teens, had as big of a psychological effect on me as the sexual abuse itself did. Additionally, my mother was always emotionally detached from me my whole life. Her distant behavior compounded the effects of what my father was doing to me. (I examine the effects of other factors which compounded the trauma of my sexual abuse in Chapter 5.)

Many people ask me how he got away with what he did to me and what his methodology was. To begin with, an abuser has to get close to the child. Pedophiles often take positions in society that allow them access to children like school teachers, athletic coaches or child care professionals. The act of pedophiles intentionally getting close to children, both physically and emotionally, is called "*grooming*". Pedophiles groom children as well as parents, building trust with parents to get close to their children. My father was obviously already close to me. He lived with me, he knew my personality and how to shape it at that young age to fit his needs. A pedophile's own children are their most easily-accessible targets and their most easily-controllable targets.

Pedophiles maintain their victim's silence with either some kind of reward, some kind of threat or both. Often, the abuser may even make a confused, impressionable child believe that he or she is not only asking for what is happening, but that they actually enjoy what was happening. If the sexual abuse is being treated as a punishment for the child, the abuser often convinces the child that he or she made it happen, that the abuse was their fault. Over the years, I have heard many twisted, clever and sinister manipulations told to children by their abusers to keep them from exposing their abusers. All of these lies told to children are obvious manipulations to adults, but children believe them.

My father was absolutely in the position of authority in our family. My mother diverted to his decisions and he was the one who handed down punishments. I would often hear from my mother that I'm going to "get it" when my father gets home. When I put the pieces together from my past, it's clear how he controlled the environment which allowed him to hide the abuse from the rest of my family.

If we could create an environment in our society today where people know how to spot both abuse victims and abusers by their behavior, we would be able to more easily spot these situations while they're occurring.

Some of the abusive signs my father exhibited were:

• Insisting on physical contact even when it made me uncomfortable. This happened when other people were around and also when we were alone. I would see him doing this to other children in public, as well, playing it off as being friendly.

• Finding a reason to walk in on me when I was undressed

in my bedroom or in the bathroom, especially when I was in the shower.

• Creating situations where he was alone with me away from the rest of the family. My father would have my mother go to church every Sunday with my older two siblings so he could stay home alone with his two toddlers.

Any one of these kinds of behaviors could be easily dismissed, but by putting all of them together, a pattern of behavior is revealed that could call into question a person's motives. I have found that listening to my intuition will either send up a red flag about a person's behavior, or calm my suspicions about them. My advice is to listen to your gut. If you suspect that an adult could be an abuser of children, take a moment to sit down and put together a simple behavior pattern on that person. There may be a simple explanation for what's happening, in which case you can comfortably dismiss it. In my experience, most people working with children actually love children in a respectful way. A little present awareness, however, could save a child from abuse.

AM I REMEMBERING IT CORRECTLY?

If you're asking yourself this question, then clearly you are having some kind of memory or memories that are making you uncomfortable. This can be a very confusing time, but take a deep breath, be brave and look your memories right in the eye. Shine a light on them and get comfortable looking at them.

One way to shine a light on them is to have a therapist guide you through the process of unpacking your memories to see what they are. Whether you go to a traditional western therapist or some kind of energy healer who does regressions, this process is worth exploring so you can look at your memories without fear of reliving them. It's the fear of reliving them that keeps them repressed.

If they are not actually memories of some kind of abuse you endured, then ask yourself what they are memories of. If you weren't abused, then find out where these memories are coming from. My advice is to dig, get to the truth and be honest with yourself. If you find out that these are not actually memories of abuse, great. And, if they're not memories of abuse, find out what is causing them. No matter what they are and what is causing them, it's something that clearly needs to be addressed because it's upsetting you. It's something that your brain is trying to bring your attention to. Be brave and honest with yourself so you can get to the truth. Whatever it is, you'll be a stronger and healthier person after you figure it out.

One of the biggest questions I had before I began going to therapy was, "if I am the victim of years of repeated sexual abuse at the hands of my own father, why don't I remember it clearly?" The answer, which I found through therapy and research, is that my mind suppressed those terrible memories and the attached emotional content in order for me to survive that time in my life. I was far too young to process the horror of what was happening, so my mind kept the memories hidden away from me. The brain's job is to protect us, and this is one way our brains do that.

Another question I had was, "I clearly remember other traumatic events in my life, like when I broke my leg, so why don't I remember the ongoing abuse?" Breaking a leg can be scary and physically painful, but sexual abuse involves complex issues of personal intimacy, consent, shame, anger, a loss of control, and other very confusing emotional trauma that a child is absolutely not equipped to handle. For me, the sexual abuse started when I was three years old. I was just learning how to communicate, how to interact with other people and just beginning to discover who I was. At that age, I was taken advantage of by a sexual predator who manipulated me into doing things that traumatized me. By hiding these memories away, my mind was doing its job to protect me and I'm glad that it did its job. Later in my life, as the memories began to come back, it was a message from my brain that it thought I was finally strong enough to deal with these memories. If memories are starting to come back for you, my advice is to consciously recognize them, but take it slowly. Take time to digest everything as it comes back to you. Write it down if you like. The more you become comfortable with looking at these newly discovered and shocking memories, the more you will continue to remember.

One of the strongest indications I had that I was abused, in addition to my memories, was that my brother, who is two years older than me, was exhibiting signs that he had also been sexually abused by my father. His symptoms and behavior were similar to what I was experiencing, and they were actually worse than mine. Adding this evidence to my own memories helped me to realize that the doubts I was having about my own memory were unwarranted. The physical manifestation of symptoms in another one of my father's children was helpful in convincing me that my suspicions were true.

WHY DID THE ABUSE HAPPEN?

When you look at the big picture, this is probably the biggest question of all. Some people who sexually abuse children recognize that it's wrong to do what they're doing and are deeply unhappy about what they're feeling and what they're doing. It doesn't keep them from doing it, but they live a life filled with guilt and shame for their actions. Other abusers believe their behavior is OK and think that what they're doing shows their love for children. Some, but not all, have been abused themselves and are acting out a repetition of the cycle. Other abusers come from other kinds of violent or unhappy family backgrounds. There are also pedophiles who do not come from abusive backgrounds, but are simply adults who are sexually attracted to prepubescent boys and girls.

All of the reasons that modern science has documented regarding why pedophiles offend, either come from educated guesswork on the part of the researcher or come from the abusers themselves; from testimony of how they feel, and why they do what they do. Upon being interviewed, some of them say that they had what they call a normal childhood. As children, they were attracted to kids their own age. But as they grew older, their sexual desires never matured along with their age and they still found sexual pleasure in thinking about prepubescent boys or girls.

At the time of my writing this book, medical research is only just beginning to tie sexual orientation of pedophiles to some kind of chemical imbalance that may be occurring while still in the womb. There also seems to be an inordinate amount of left-handed pedophiles, which may seem unrelated, but the statistics suggests something meaningful. Normally 8% of men are non-right-handed, but 30% of pedophiles are left handed. This shows a right brain dominance at a high enough frequency to be compared to disorders like schizophrenia and autism. This is a strong argument that pedophilia is a condition which begins when the brain is forming in the womb.

This desire may exist in an uncontrollable way, but acting on it is another matter. Many pedophiles do act on their attraction to children, becoming child molesters, but many do not. Accurate numbers are currently impossible to acquire, but a seemingly huge number of pedophiles resist their sexual orientation, living both in celibacy and in secret. In recent years, websites for non-offending pedophiles have appeared and their memberships are growing into the thousands. Interviews with these people reveal that their sexual attraction and desire to children can be compared, in its strength, to what "normal" people experience in their sexual attraction to other adults. Pedophiles who I've interviewed say that they feel cursed with an attraction to children and, if there were a pill they could take to "cure" them of their desires, they would take it without hesitation. The emergence of non-offending pedophiles is currently another extremely emotional and polarized topic of debate.

It's often said that pedophiles abuse children because they, themselves, were abused as children. One of my biggest concerns for years, was that I would follow in my father's footsteps and abuse children, simply because I was his son. All my life, when I found myself around children - especially children who were the same age as me when I was abused - my knee-jerk reaction was to avoid them. I have never been sexually attracted to children, but being around them always made me uncomfortable. Until my memories resurfaced, I never understood why. I have since abandoned that fear. I am my own person with my own ability to reason and decide what is best for me and for others. Today, when I see children, my heart shines with love and respect for them. Seeing children makes me want to support them in having the happy, healthy childhood that I was not afforded.

If it was an abusive past that made my father decide to do what he did, then I've broken that generational chain by wanting to do the exact opposite. If my father was not sexually abused as a child and simply was sexually attracted to children because that's who he was, then I did not receive that trait from him. Thanks to very intentional self-examination, I know who I am as an adult and I am not frightened of myself.

Anyone who uses children for their own sexual desires is doing so without consent of that child. A child can not legally or morally consent to having any kind of sexual relations with and adult. The adult abuser of children is breaking the law, is breaking trust and is putting his or her own needs above all others. The truth in my case is that I will never know exactly why my abuse happened. For the purposes of my recovery, it's ultimately irrelevant why it happened as long as I realize that it did not happen because of anything I did. I am not to blame. I didn't ask for it. At three years old, I did not approach my father and ask him to have sex with me. In no way at all is anything that happened, my fault. And, as a child, I didn't "let" this happen. No child who is the victim of abuse is to blame for their abuse.

I believe that part of why I was sexually abused as a child is because my father had no option for therapy to try and deal with this desires. Pedophilia has been socially stigmatized to the point of accepted group hatred. It is the go-to reaction of our society that pedophiles deserve the worst of punishments. This is an unconscious group mentality that tends to not look at individual situations and really only fosters solidarity through vocalizing hatred. Society's only current solution to childhood sexual abuse is the most severe punishment after the abuse has happened.

In this kind of environment of mass hate, lines get blurred and people who have not broken the law get targeted. If we, as a society, create an environment that would allow pedophiles to come forward for treatment as an alternative to abusing children, it would create a possibility – even a probability – for prevention. This would surely benefit all of us.

Back in the 1970's, in that small, rural Oklahoma town, if my father had lived in a society where he was taught to recognize his tendency toward pedophilia as a treatable condition, and was afforded a treatment center for his condition, I may never have been abused. I'm not condoning what my father did, but after years of looking at this issue from every possible angle, I've realized from my abuser's point of view, that he felt like he really didn't have anywhere to turn for help with this publically-condemned perversion. Those of us who are recovering from abuse, who are now coming forward to talk about it, are creating a public conversation around pedophilia, where there previously was none, fueling positive change.

By examining the problem of pedophilia in an honest way, we can hopefully help to make a change in society by creating resources for childhood sexual abuse victims and also for potential offenders. These websites, where self-identified, non-offending pedophiles can come forward, is a first step in this process of creating resources for potential offenders. In order for the social stigma of pedophilia to change, we must reach a point when someone can raise their hand, stand up and say, "I'm a pedophile who doesn't want to offend", and people will want to help them, instead of hang them.

DO I REALLY WANT TO KNOW THE TRUTH?

When I first started to realize that a sexual relationship with my own father was actually a part of my past, I was terrified. The thoughts were shocking, nauseating, and confusing. Part of me thought that if I just didn't think about it, I could move forward with my life and everything would be fine. I actually tried that for years and eventually learned that refusing to deal with the memories that were surfacing, was not an option. Once they came up, the memories refused to stay buried. I decided to take a leap. As scary and disgusting as it was, I decided to become honest with myself about what had happened to me.

One of the first things I realized was that I was currently being affected by something that happened to me decades ago. As I looked at my current self, I noticed I was exhibiting certain behaviors that were making me feel weak and disempowered. Prior to this realization, I would never have thought of my behavior as weak, powerless, or small. If someone had told me that I was disempowered or weak, I would have quickly disagreed with them. My advice is, if you're not used to honestly looking at your own behavior, it can be challenging, but definitely not impossible. If you need a little help with your own self-examination, then you can practice by observing other people around you. Practice looking at their behaviors and being honest about what you see. Don't attach judgmental words to what that person is doing, just observe and identify behavior. For example, it can be easy to see when someone else is acting out of fear, is being prejudiced in their opinions, or getting overtly angry about something very specific. Consciously work on seeing other people's responses in certain situations and certain behaviors will begin to stand out.

You might say to yourself, "he always asks my opinion about something instead of making a decision for himself", or, "She really gets very upset or defensive when I mention this certain thing". As you begin to get good at identifying these disempowering behaviors, then just take that practice and apply it to yourself. It takes a little practice and, again, honesty is key. Pretty soon, you're seeing behaviors in yourself that may be hard to admit, but which will benefit you to notice and possibly change.

Through this practice, I learned that the abuse from my childhood was still effecting and controlling my current behavior as an adult. I was exhibiting reduced self worth, submissiveness, shame and inappropriate levels of anger in certain situations. For example, I would ask other people's opinions on how to do something instead of making up my own mind. I would settle for something less than I wanted because I didn't think I was worthy of something better. These newly-recognized behaviors were now obvious to me and they were not healthy for me. But, this was ultimately good news because I could now see that my abusive past was the source of these current, negative behaviors. I realized that, to let them go, I would have to shine a light on my memories and not be afraid of them anymore. I would have to drag the monster out of the dark closet and into the light where it has no power. This scary thing from my past had at least some control over my current life, and I was not willing to let that continue. I was not willing to live with the side effects of this abuse any longer. These memories that were surfacing now in my life were a message to me, a catalyst, that I was ready to heal and become strong again, instead of continuing to be afraid, submissive and not living to my potential.

If you have been sexually abused and you haven't healed from it, you will find some effects of that abuse showing up in your current life if you look for them. (Chapter 4 discusses examples of some of these effects so you can more easily recognize them.) If you're noticing negative behavior patterns in yourself, it's possible that an abusive or traumatic situation is the root cause of those behaviors. This is a huge realization because you can now stop blaming yourself for acting in ways that you don't like.

Take time to digest this massive realization in a self-loving way. Go easy on yourself and congratulate yourself for becoming aware. This is an essential, foundational realization, that must happen to make forward progress in your recovery. Facing the truth of your abusive past, will only help improve your current life.

These behaviors could be effects of the sexual abuse you

endured, or it could be side effects of an associated event in your life that happened along with the abuse. It's up to you to change how you're behaving so that you can be happy. Some people metaphorically say that, to heal from a wound you have to leave it alone. I believe that you have to clean that wound out first, so it can heal properly. To change the behaviors you're exhibiting that you don't like, you have to go to the source and disempower it, so you can become empowered. Right now, it has the power, and you will have to commit to taking it back.

SELF HONESTY

The only way to heal from the devastating effects of sexual abuse is by honest self-examination. For those of us who have repressed memories of our abuse, being honest with ourselves can be a difficult thing to learn, and here's why. Up until our memories started to resurface, our subconscious minds have been telling us that the abuse did not happen. Our minds have been doing that because we were not strong enough to deal with it at the time. Our brains have literally been lying to us since the abuse happened – possibly for many years. Knowing this, we should not only go easy on ourselves in the way of judgment, but we should be proud of our minds for coming up with a way to be able to live through what happened. Lying to ourselves was our mind's way of protecting us by hiding the memories and the pain. The memories are not gone - they're still there, they are just cleverly hidden. There was a time when hiding these memories helped us to survive, but now we don't need that dishonesty anymore. We're strong adults who now have the ability to deal with whatever comes at us. This is why painful memories, feelings and suspicions have decided to surface, because now we have the strength to deal with them. This is the moment in our lives that we can begin to take the power away from our abuser, who stole it from us during the abuse, and we can give it back to ourselves. In that way, the memories that are now resurfacing are actually a gift. They are an opportunity to expand and grow stronger.

Your abuser may also have taught you – or forced you – to lie to other people about what happened. If this went on for years, then you've been continually lying to others in order to survive the situation. As much energy as it takes to lie when you want to, it's even more demanding and difficult to lie when you don't want to – or are being forced to. This is a traumatic situation in itself. Realizing that you may have become a habitual liar can be difficult to admit, but realizing that it's not your fault – that it was a survival mechanism of the mind – can help you to release it and come gently back to being the honest person that you naturally are.

Once I realized that I had been lying to myself about the abuse that had happened, I also noticed I was lying to myself about all sorts of things. I was also currently lying to other people in my life – mostly about small things – in order to "protect myself" in many different ways. It became obvious that lying to protect myself had become a subconscious habit throughout my life. This is a common, ongoing side effect of this kind of abuse. It was important to realize that becoming someone who told so many habitual lies was not my fault. Slowly, bit by bit, I recognized these little lies in my life and became more honest with myself about everything I was feeling, everything I was doing and it opened up a dialog with myself that was incredibly empowering. I remember the day that I decided to start being honest about everything with everyone in my life. I decided to go cold turkey and stop lying about anything. This immediately changed how I communicated with everyone. I stopped saying things like, "No, I never got your email". Instead I simply said, "Yes, I got your email, I just haven't responded to it yet". I took time to think of what I wanted to say before I answered other people's questions and, in response, I found that people were appreciating my attitude.

If you find that you've been lying to other people, and you don't want to set the record straight with them for fear of losing them as friends, my advice is to go ahead, start a dialog with them and tell them the truth. This kind of bold behavior not only releases you from continued lying, it also lets you know who your friends really are. If people find out that you're recovering from sexual abuse and that you are bravely working through these issues, they will either understand and support you, or they will turn their back on you which means they are not your friends anyway. It has been said that the truth will set you free and I've found that to absolutely be true. The healing process will simply not work unless you are brutally honest with yourself. Be brave. Be honest. Make honesty your new habit. You've already been through the worst of it. Now is the time for honesty and healing.

Being honest with myself – and with others – is something that my abuser took away from me, it's the first thing on my healing journey that I took back, and it's made all the difference. Our brains have been lying to us, to protect us for so long, but the practice of continuously lying drains us of our vital energy, as a burden that we carry around with us. Since I stopped all the lying in my life, I have reclaimed all of that energy that I was expending on lying. I feel lighter, stronger and full of confidence. And I want the same for you.

WHAT ABOUT THE GOOD MEMORIES I HAVE?

Just because you have good memories about your abuser doesn't mean that the abuse didn't happen. Both the good and bad memories can be true; one does not negate the other. Regarding my father, I have wonderful memories of one of my brothers and I going to the lake with my father on Saturdays in the summer. We would sing all the way there and then sail boats and paddle canoes around the lake as a team. These great memories are absolutely contradictory to the memories I have of the sexual abuse. Ultimately the good memories have nothing to do with what happened when I was alone with my father in his bedroom, in the shower, or any of the other places he abused me. One of the things I've heard from abuse survivors is that they somehow believe that because they have good memories, that the bad memories of the abuse could not have happened. This is simply denial of what happened.

Adults who sexually abuse children are people who wear masks of deceit. To do this immoral and illegal thing, my father lied to those around him constantly and, ultimately in my father's case, he was lying to himself as well. Abusers are manipulators. One possibility is that your abuser spent time creating good memories with you to somehow counteract the fact that he/she was abusing you. I believe that my father did wonderful things with us kids because part of him actually wanted to be a good father. I think he was conflicted about the abuse he was inflicting on me during those other times when we were alone.

Whatever your abuser's motivations may have been, the

bottom line is that a good memory does not mean that a bad memory is not valid or real. My advice is to simply be as honest with yourself as you can be. If you have good memories and bad memories, respect them both. If you're remembering them both, then they both happened.

WHAT DO I DO NOW?

If you are currently in a sexual abuse situation, my obvious advice is to get out of it. If you can't do that on your own, then get immediate help. I suggest RAINN.org as a first step. They will listen to you without judgment and can advise you on reporting your abuser. They can guide you to legal advice for your specific state and they offer an enormous variety of options to help your recovery. They are the people I recommend that you contact to help you think through how to proceed with your immediate next steps.

If you are currently not in an abuse situation, but are dealing with the effects of past abuse, then you have some choices to make on how you would like to proceed.

Whether you are struggling to remember what happened to you or not, you have been honest enough with yourself to become aware of the memories and look at them, so you've started to reclaim your self-honesty. You are also now reading this book which means you've already started your journey of recovery. My advice is to keep going. Keep being honest with yourself and it will inevitably take you to a better place. Ask yourself how you feel. Ask yourself how you WANT to feel. This is your journey and your life. You can make it whatever you want it to be. When I was in this position, the next thing I did after the realization of my abuse was to reach out and start talking to friends who I thought could help me.

CHUCK TYLER

CHAPTER 2

CREATING A SUPPORT SYSTEM

"Remember, you don't need a certain number of friends,
just a number of friends you can be certain of."

- Unknown

WHY DO I NEED A SUPPORT SYSTEM?

Creating a personal support system will give you outside eyes on your situation. It will give you alternate perspectives that you may not be able to see because you're so far inside of what's happening to you. It will also benefit you to surround yourself with people who care about you, especially when you're abuser may have trained you not to care about yourself. There was a lot going on inside my head and heart during those early months of realization. I felt like it was impossible to sort it all out, which left me stuck in a rut of seeing everything the same way over and over again. I kept coming to the same dead-end conclusions and I needed some kind of helpful shift. I really needed outside perspectives. I was fortunate enough to already have a couple of people in my life who knew me and truly cared about me. I shared my situation with them, asked them to be part of my support system and they agreed. It was their perspectives and advice, blended with honestly listening to my own intuition, that shifted me out of my rut and helped guide me along a path which ultimately led me to where I am today.

I personally believe that we are all here on this planet to help each other, especially when dealing with trauma that skews our internal perspectives so much. A support system gives you a cheering section to help keep you going on your path of recovery. Whenever I began to slip into a depressive state, my friends who were my support would point it out to me. I didn't notice it, but they did, and they said something to me. This outside help, combined with focused self honesty, helped me to see whether I was actually healing or avoiding healing. It also helped me to see what negative behaviors I was exhibiting, that I could not realize on my own. These little realizations along the way helped keep me on course. My support system was very valuable in helping me steadily reclaim my power, and gain clarity regarding my childhood. It's clear to me now that talking with my dedicated support system showed me what life could be like if I moved beyond my abuse by working through it and not letting it effect me anymore.

Talking to other people who have worked through the effects of childhood sexual abuse is definitely helpful. But talking to people who have NOT been abused also gives you a new perspective on what a life can look like without abuse. When you are an abuse survivor, and you talk to people who have not been abused, their stories of growing up are very different from yours. Their stories probably don't include being frightened to go to the bathroom at home or to go to sleep at night for fear of someone coming in. If you grew up with sexual trauma, like I did, you don't really know anything else. Abuse was part of my life like eating and sleeping. Talking through my own life situations with someone who did NOT grow up with that kind of abuse, and listening to their shared stories of growing up, helped me to experience a new way of looking at being alive.

Once you are aware of that different experience and really understand it as much as you can (without having experienced it yourself), you can decide to take your life into a direction that incorporates elements of the other life that appeals to you. You can define your own life as one that is guided by your own intentions instead of by past experiences.

Overall, a caring support system will keep you from going down this path or recovery alone. For me, alone was what I was used to. I was only comfortable watching my own back. A support system took me out of that solitary life and helped me begin to trust other people again.

WHO SHOULD I TURN TO FOR SUPPORT?

Turn to someone you trust. Not someone who simply says you can trust them, but someone you trust from your heart. Turn to someone who you feel genuinely cares about your well-being. If you don't have someone in your life that fits that description, get online and find a support group for sexual abuse survivors. The support you find in friends is different from what you will find in support group members, but when you're at the very beginning of building a support team, either one of these two options is a great starting point. The reason why I say they are different, is because friends or loved ones who care about you are focused on your well-being because they know you. They know your history, they know your story, they want you to be well, and they'll help you from that perspective. By comparison, a support group relates to you because you are also an abuse survivor, so they will initially approach you in that way. They will talk to you from a perspective of being able to relate directly to the abuse effects that you're dealing with.

When my memories started coming back to me in my late twenties, one of my first reactions was to reach out and talk to someone about it. The morning after I admitted to myself that the memories were real, I sat down with the woman I was in a relationship with and told her about the confusing thoughts I was having. I thought I was abused by my father and, somehow because of that, I thought I was now attracted to men. She was very upset and hurt, I was very confused and lost, and the situation quickly ended our relationship.

The first person outside of my relationship I decided to open up to was a work colleague who was also a good friend. I always looked up to her as a strong person who always spoke her mind without fear of repercussion. She was also openly gay, which somehow made me feel more comfortable talking to her about a sexual topic that is stigmatized in our society. I took her to lunch and told her about both the seemingly homosexual thoughts I had been having, and also about the abuse that I thought I was remembering from my childhood. After a minute of thought, she put down her fork, leaned across the table and quietly told me two things. First of all, I should realize that I was under no obligation to ever tell anyone anything. This was nobody else's business. It was my decision what to share, when to share it, and with whom to share it. The second thing she told me was to immediately create a support system of trusted friends and/or family who could help me while I was sorting all of this out. In retrospect, this was the best advice anyone had ever given me up to that point in my life. It filled me with inner strength, possibly for the first time in my life, and I held onto this advice as my first guidepost through my recovery process.

When I felt it was time to talk to my family about it, I let my intuition guide me. I have three older siblings. My parents initially had two children, a boy and a girl, who were about two years apart. Then they waited eight years and had two more boys, again about two years apart. I'm the youngest of all four. When I decided to start reaching out to the immediate members of my family about what happened, my gut told me not to talk to my mother. It also told me not to reach out to my brother who was closest in age to me. I didn't know why at the time but, once I started to put the pieces together, it seemed obvious to me that my older brother who was closest to me in age, had also been sexually abused by my father.

I called my sister and eldest brother and spoke to each of them separately about what I was going through. My sister, the oldest of all of us, was someone I would always turn to for advice when I was growing up. Her response to my story was that she didn't believe that our father could have done that to me, and that I must just be either confused or subconsciously making it up. She basically rejected everything I was telling her. As time went on, I spoke to her less and less and today I have no communication with her at all.

I have learned that when I share the story of my abuse with people, it acts like a filter. Some people immediately pass through the filter and become supportive of my situation. These are the people I have decided to keep in my life. Other people either didn't believe what I was saying, or they wanted nothing to do with me after I shared my story with them. These are the people I decided to let fade away out of my life, no matter who they were.

When I reached out to my oldest brother, he listened and accepted what I had to say. He told me that he personally had no sexually abusive experiences with my father, but he didn't discount what I told him. He then told me that he loved me and that he would always be there for me to support me however I needed it. To this day, he's the only member of my family that I have any communication with. In fact, years later, I asked him to be the best man at my wedding.

In addition to my work colleague who I first opened up to and two of my siblings, I shared my situation with a few trusted friends who ended up standing by me and supporting me. I also shared my story with a couple of friends who just quietly nodded as I spoke. After that, almost instantly, they quietly drifted out of my life and I never saw them again. I really thought these "friends" who faded away were close friends, but I was mistaken. (I discuss old friends, new friends and the changing definition of what friends are in later chapters.)

If you don't have close friends or family members that you are comfortable reaching out to, then I highly recommend joining a support group. This is very different than speaking with close friends who were not abused, and it is incredibly helpful. Your situation is exactly what these kinds of groups are designed for. They will welcome you into a community of people who went through what you did. A simple internet search for support groups in your area that help your exact abuse situation will give you options. If you don't find a support group in your area, or that you're comfortable with, I currently do online sessions via my website, to help close the gap for this very issue.

There are groups that meet online using web cameras in an online group format. I have done this before and it's a gentle first step into this process. My personal feeling, however, is that anything online is a detached, watered-down version of spending time with another human being. There is no online group situation that is more nurturing and empowering than physically being in a room with other people in your same situation. The energy in a live support group is incomparable. I recommend this over the online groups, even if you have to commute to get to one.

For the rest of my life, I will remember going to my first support group. I initially called the organization on the phone, then I signed up online and finally had to meet with the moderator of the group before I was allowed to actually join. It felt like a very professional and secure process and it made me feel safe. The first night I walked into that meeting room, I sat down in one of the folding chairs that was placed in a circle and I looked around at the other eight men. We were all childhood sexual abuse survivors who were abused by men, mostly by our fathers. Without a word, we all just gently smiled and nodded at each other. It was the single most powerful moment in my journey of recovery. I knew, as did the others in that group, that we had a safe place to come and talk about what happened. We knew that we would all be believed and supported.

A trained facilitator in the group guided us through a format of the meeting, reading through the rules of discretion, guiding us to choose the topics of discussion and keeping us on track with the conversation. The discussion was driven by the attendees and not the facilitator, which was empowering as well. We met once a week very discreetly in a small classroom of a community college after hours. Instead of having to explain my situation, my feelings, and my behavior to someone who had never been through it, these support groups suddenly put me into a room full of people who all instantly understood. They could give me *their* perspectives on *my* situation. I was no longer alone.

I eventually became a member of two support groups that were comprised completely of men who were abused as children by adult men. Again, most of these men were sexually abused by their fathers. Support groups did wonders for the advancement of my recovery and I absolutely recommend them. I now even host my own local support group in my town.

One thing to be aware of, however, is to let group therapy be a step on your journey of recovery, not a destination. I have known people who put their energy *only* into group therapy and who didn't pursue any other kind of forward movement on their journey of recovery. They used the group environment for commiseration, which is something that can feel like a destination because it is a safe place compared to where they had been since their abuse. Don't let group therapy, or any step on your journey, be a pothole on your path where you get stuck. Group therapy is a wonderful supplement to creating a support system of friends as well as a regular therapist.

HOW MUCH SHOULD I SHARE WITH PEOPLE?

For the first few years after my memories came back, I

said nothing and lived mostly in a kind-of confused silence. When I finally did become vocal, it felt embarrassing on multiple levels. Talking about it felt like an invasion of my personal, intimate history. Also, the fact that I had very little memory of the details, meant that I couldn't answer the questions that people were asking me about it. Even though hearing myself talking about it out loud felt good, it became obvious that I wasn't quite ready to share with confidence, after testing the water. I realize now that I was still in the early stages of processing not only what happened, but the effects that the abuse had on my personality and my behavior. I was exploring the tip of an iceberg.

The fact that I was embarrassed about it, was also an indication that I felt, on some level, responsible for what happened. This perspective finally changed but, at the time, I kept everything inside until I understood more about what I was going through. My journey of recovery at that stage was largely a solitary one. Deciding what to share, and with whom to share it, took some time.

At this stage, my favorite thing to say was, "I'm not comfortable talking about it yet". This is a great go-to statement to have in your back pocket when someone surprises you with a personal question. I know now that, anybody who truly cares about you, will respect that statement. It has also become crystal clear that anyone who continues to push you after you say you're not comfortable talking about it, obviously doesn't care about you.

You may be surprised to find that some friends you talk to, will ask for the intimate gory details of the abuse, not because they care about your well-being, but because they want something to gossip about or are craving a story with some shock value. My advice is to listen to your gut with how much you share with people. Your intuition will let you know when you're ready to talk, how much to share, and with whom to share it. As a general rule, I would suggest that, in the beginning, the intimate details of your story should be reserved for your therapist, group therapy with other survivors, and not open conversation with friends.

DOES SHARING MY STORY REALLY HELP?

Absolutely. When you're ready to talk, definitely start talking. Sharing your story with another person, or with a group, helps in different ways. First of all, it's empowering to say it out loud and to hear yourself say it! Whenever you transform what you are feeling inside into words and then speak them out loud, you are taking energy and turning it into something physical as you say it. It makes your recovery physically real. When you talk about how you're working your way through it, no matter what stage of the healing process you are in, you BECOME your story of healing. You become the person that is overcoming it.

Secondly, as you describe to people how you are overcoming it, you become an inspiration to them. I started talking to people about my abuse for my own benefit, but the surprise for me was that they were benefiting from it, too. I could see it in their faces as I talked with them. Both of these results will give you strength by helping you realize how far you've come, how strong you are and how you are now shining like a light as an inspiration to others.

SUPPORT YOURSELF

The person who is going to be supporting you the most is yourself. Start learning what it means to be your own best friend. Practice it. As you stop lying to yourself about what happened, it will begin to open up a relationship of trust with yourself. The truth is the truth. Face it and then be there for yourself when it gets ugly. Your body knows you're strong enough to handle this acceptance, that's why the memories are coming back. Trust your body's decision and be proud that you're dealing with it, and be proud of yourself of how strong you are. When you're no longer living the lie, you're becoming the "you" that was suppressed before the abuse happened. You're beginning to reclaim yourself. You're beginning to take it all back.

As I was going through the early stages of my recovery, I received a simple and powerful piece of advice from a trusted friend of mine. She knew what I was going through and she was absolutely part of my support system. I was telling her about how hard I was trying to make someone happy at my job, when she stopped me and said, "why don't you point that big, loving heart at yourself?". That comment immediately brought me to tears. I realized right there that, even though I had some people around me who cared about me and who were helping to support me, I needed to be my own best friend first. Being my own best friend meant taking the time to do caring things for myself. Those things I was so willing to do for other people, I needed to do those for myself. (A wonderful story note here is that this supportive friend of mine is now my wife!)

Some people like to write in a journal as a way of working through things. If writing your story down empowers you, I definitely recommend it. I've seen it help others. I tried journaling, but was never totally comfortable with it. I have a very fast working brain and writing in a journal – or even typing – could never keep up with how fast my brain rockets down the road from thought to thought. A therapist might tell me that journaling is a way to slow down and really look at what I'm thinking, but I have made it to where I am today without journaling. I suppose the fact that I've written a book about my journey through recovery is proof that I am finally comfortable writing about what happened.

I had reached a point where talking to my supportive friends about my past was somehow not enough. I was pleasantly surprised to realize that I wanted a deeper conversation, but I didn't want to always be talking about sexual abuse when I was with my friends. I had come to a turning point in my recovery. I felt like I was ready to talk to a professional. That's when I decided to move into regular therapy.

CHAPTER 3

THERAPY AND THERAPISTS

"You are not broken,
you are breaking through."

- Alex Myles

WHAT IS THERAPY AND DO I REALLY NEED IT?

Therapy generally consists of sitting and talking with someone who has been trained to sit and listen to you without judgment and then give you options on which way you can go to work through your problems. Some therapists specialize in specific issues and others are ready to help anyone with anything they have to work through. You can expect one-hour sessions with varied prices depending on where you live, with the first session typically being spent on getting to know each other. Going to see a therapist is very specific and intentional act. In that way, I think it's much more powerful than anything you can do on your own. I know many people who have been through therapy and not one of them has ever said, "Wow, I really wasted my money on therapy", or, "I got nothing out of it". The truth is that you will never know if therapy is right for you until you go and try it for yourself.

At the very beginning of my recovery, when the memories first started to come back, therapy helped me to build a foundation for the rest of my recovery. The realization I had in my basement, that I was sexually abused by my father, was devastating and I needed someone to talk to. Even if you remember your own abuse situation, and you don't have suppressed memories like I did, therapy can give you a roadmap to different recovery paths to choose.

Before this, I had been to a therapist once before in my life and it was a bad experience. I had been having concentration issues in college and the therapist I visited quickly diagnosed me with ADHD. He prescribed Ritalin for me and shuffled me out the door. My view of western psychology was based on that one experience; treat the symptom with prescription medication and move on. In retrospect, this was not the best introduction into the world of therapy.

Years later, realizing I was sexually abused, I had hesitations for visiting a therapist again; I didn't want to go to a therapist just to become medicated. What I did want was answers to some frightening questions. And then, after I got those answers, I wanted guidance on what to do next. My small network of friends and family were there to support me, but I felt it was time for outside eyes and a professional's opinion. Even if I didn't agree or accept what a therapist had to say, I was not only willing to hear it,

I wanted to hear it.

In the small mountain town of Colorado, were I was living at the time, skimming through the Therapist section of the Yellow Pages gave me some slim pickings. Back then, the internet is not what it is today so my resources were limited. I ended up choosing someone simply because he had an appointment available and, in retrospect, he was not very good. I would probably have found more direct and effective help by choosing a therapist in a nearby larger city, and then commuting to my sessions. Nonetheless, after doing some simple work with this mediocre, small-town therapist, during just a couple of visits, I achieved some surprisingly effective results. Over the course of several years, different therapists introduced me to several techniques for memory recovery, all of which gently brought back memories and helped me to put pieces together that I would not have been able to assemble otherwise. For me, therapy was a successful stepping stone on my journey to recovery. I recommend trying it, even if only to solidly decide that it's not for you.

HOW DO I CHOOSE A THERAPIST?

The first thing I would suggest is to look for someone who has expertise in whatever your particular abuse situation was. The first therapist I chose did not focus on childhood sexual abuse and he still was able to help me, if only just to get me started. Still, if I had it to do over again, I would have chosen a specialist in my field. If you find a therapist who specializes in your specific issue and it requires you to commute to get there, I think that it's worth the drive. One thing to remember is that you don't have to be dedicated to one therapist. If you don't feel comfortable with your first therapist, just try another one. You don't owe any of them an explanation. If they're pushy, then they don't have your best interests in mind. I had one therapist tell me that I had to sign up for sixteen sessions minimum and then pay for half of all of them up front! I never went back to her and never called her again. Remember, this is not about them, it's about you.

An important decision for me was choosing either a male or female therapist. Since my abuse situation involved a man abusing a boy, I thought talking with a male therapist made sense. Over the years I have been to many therapists and have found that I prefer talking with a woman. My biggest breakthroughs have been from working with a female therapist, but it all stemmed from the work I did with that first male therapist who, like I said, wasn't that good.

If you're new to therapy, and you're open to it, I think just about any therapy at first is going to help. Once you're in motion, you can change course at any time. As I have said, a therapist is a person who is not there to judge you, who is going to listen to what you have to say and give you advice on how to move forward with recovery. All of that is ultimately helpful. There are as many different kinds of therapists in the world as there are people, so don't let a bad experience with one therapist keep you from trying others. Your relationship with your therapist is a lot like any other relationship in your life. It will be more effective if you are comfortable with the person you choose.

WHAT ARE THE BENEFITS OF THERAPY?

Therapists ask questions that you don't ask yourself. They ask you direct questions and usually they are tough questions. Be honest when you answer them. Maybe you're scared to ask yourself certain questions or maybe you just don't know what to ask yourself. Just be honest when you answer them. This person is not just a second set of eyes on your situation, they are a trained second set of eyes. What they say WILL help you... if you're honest. Go into a therapy session ready to share everything with them. Hold nothing back. Dump it all out into their lap and let them look at it and give you whatever advice they can.

Be ready and willing to commit to a of couple sessions, not just one. (You shouldn't have to pre-pay for any of them.) Recurring therapy sessions build on themselves, to move forward. Many times I would walk out of my therapist's office thinking it was a so-so session and I was not sure if I got anything out of it. Then, through the course of my daily life, I would come across a situation that would spark something my therapist said to me the day before, and I would have an insight. A little light would come on and I would make a connection that would be helpful to my recovery. Those are the moments of moving forward that kept me going back to therapy.

Setting an intention to heal yourself is powerful and going to a therapist is a physical manifestation of that intention. Make time, put forth the effort and get into an honest, healing mindset on a regular basis, then bring that into your therapy sessions. I found that going to a one hour session with a therapist always, always helped – as long as I was honest when I walked into their office. I was going there to search for the truth and, although I didn't know what I would find, I knew that holding back would not get me there. Again, I can't say it enough, honesty is the key.

ARE THERE DRAWBACKS TO THERAPY?

Overall, therapy has been a positive force in my life, but there were some awkward moments. My first therapist, like I said, was not that good. I think he simply wasn't that experienced. I didn't realize he wasn't that good until later, when I had other therapists to compare him to. Other therapists, later in my life, knew how to ask very specific questions that dug right to the heart of the topic. Also, these better therapists did so in such a way that didn't seem pushy or invasive. Looking back in comparison, that first therapist made me work harder to move forward and maybe that was a good thing. Maybe his style was not compatible with my personality. Let your gut tell you if you're compatible with your therapist. You may spend some time and money finding the right one, but when you do, it will be worth the effort.

Interesting to note that, of all the therapists I've ever had, not one of them had ever personally been sexually abused. I know this because I asked each one of them. Not only was I hoping to find someone with a specialty with childhood sexual abuse, but also someone with my highly specific circumstances of being sexually abused by a biological parent. I never found that specific therapist, but I did find healing through the work I did with my therapists.

After all the research I've done since my early days of

therapy, I've come to learn that, at some point in their lives, one in three women are sexually abused as children and one in six men are sexually abused as children. And those are just the ones who admit it to the person taking the survey, so those numbers are undoubtedly higher. With that statistic in mind, I suppose any or all of my therapists could have been abused and just didn't tell me about it. If that was the case, then maybe they're not admitting it to themselves or maybe they figured it was just none of my business. I initially thought that any therapist who had not gone through what I had gone through was no better to me than spending time reading a textbook. Over time, I learned that all therapists, especially the childhood sexual abuse specialists, worked with people in my position all of the time, and talking with them helped me make positive movement with my recovery.

WHAT TYPES OF TREATMENT CAN I EXPECT?

There are a few treatments that specifically helped me break through some barriers, allowing me to have some realizations about what happened to me. First and foremost, is just talking about it. Expect to talk with your therapist. Again, be honest and forthcoming. Don't be surprised if this brings up emotional reactions in yourself, and don't be scared of these emotions. The therapist's office is a safe place to express yourself. Be willing to cry, get angry, get frustrated, be regretful – let all of these things out in an honest way. Every therapist office has a box of tissues on the table.

It was only after a certain amount of talking that I moved onto specific treatments with my therapists. I discuss a few of them here, but do your own research and try different things for yourself. Everyone is different and we all respond in different ways to different treatments.

The first treatment I underwent was called EMDR, or Eye Movement Desensitization and Reprocessing. This was very effective for me and brought up some of the first old memories that I had suppressed. It was through EMDR that I found enough "proof" for myself that the abuse actually happened and was not just a figment of my imagination. When I reached the point that I knew for certain that the abuse from my past was real, my therapist stopped and gave me a choice. He said I could continue on and recover more old memories, or I could step back and take some time to process the fact that the sexual abuse was real. At the time, I chose to stop my therapy for a while. I didn't return to it until years later.

Another treatment I chose was Applied Kinesiology, otherwise known as AK or "Muscle Testing". It's a process through which the therapist has you hold out your arm, close your eyes and then asks you a question. When you answer the question, the therapist then presses down on your arm and, based on the amount of resistance your body puts forth against the pressure, they can determine certain things about that topic. The idea is that your body subconsciously knows the answer to the question even if your conscious mind does not, and it communicates by either staying strong or becoming weak to the pressure on your arm. People seem to love arguing about how Muscle Testing is either helpful or fraudulent. I'm telling you that it worked for me and helped me move forward on my journey of recovery. From my perspective, anyone who has had no success with a certain kind of treatment simply needs to choose a different treatment for what they're trying to achieve.

Later I underwent a "regression", which I've also heard

referred to as a "hypnotic regression". This was a three-hour guided meditation and was very similar to being slightly hypnotized. I sat in a comfortable chair with my eyes closed, in a quiet room in my therapist's home. She talked me through a guided meditation which took me back to whatever memories I was ready to access. Her assistant made notes during the entire process and I actually recorded a video of the treatment for my own reference. A guided regression is a very comfortable way to look back and it brought up some memories that I feel like I would not have been able to access otherwise. If things started to get too intense, the therapist would talk me back out of the situation and we would go somewhere else with the guided meditation. I also had complete control over it myself and could back out of whatever I did not like. The truth is that, even though I experienced uncomfortable images and feelings during the regression, I didn't WANT to back out. I felt like an observer during the process, (as if I were standing in the room, but not actively involved) and I was not overwhelmed by any of it. Overall, this was a safe, comfortable process which yielded great results and I recommend it.

Finally, I have to mention an experience I had outside

of traditional therapy. It was during my Yoga teacher training. I attended a thirty two day ashram-style immersion course in which I studied Hatha Yoga, Ayurvedic medicine and other Vedic studies like Astrology. It was a very intense immersion course with some days lasting as long as fifteen hours. During one week of the training, we practiced a Yogic cleansing ritual known as "Kunjala" or "Kunjal Kriya". It is performed by drinking sixty four ounces of warm salt water and then regurgitating it. (It is supposed to be performed under trained supervision.) It is meant to cleanse the stomach and digestive tract, but we were told that it would also bring up past emotional issues that our bodies wanted us to deal with. During my training, we performed Kunjala every morning for one week. After I performed my first Kunjala of the week, I immediately fell into a profound depression for about two hours. I didn't want to speak and I just stared at things blankly. Finally, I spontaneously turned to one of my fellow yoga students, collapsed into her arms and started crying like I hadn't cried in years. A couple of the other students came over and held me as I cried. All of us students had similar experiences that week and we were all very supportive of each other. It actually happened to me again a couple days later in the middle of one of my classes.

After some very focused examination, what was happening to me during Kunjala was that I was crying about my childhood. I realized that I had spent years holding all my sadness inside, hiding it from everyone, and although I made progress in therapy, I never allowed any emotion to show up until this point. I was ultimately hiding my emotions from myself. I had never acknowledged to myself how terrible the sexual abuse experience was, or any of the other contributing factors. I had never "cried for myself". This week of Kunjala was the moment in my life that all of it surprisingly came to the surface. I let it all out and, afterwards, I felt light and free.

CHUCK TYLER

CHAPTER 4

THE EFFECTS OF ABUSE

"Shame is the lie
someone told you about yourself."

- Anais Nin

MEMORY LOSS AND CONFUSION

The first and most shocking element to my recovery journey was discovering that I had suppressed memories. When images and thoughts of sexual abuse from my own past began to surface, it was difficult to accept that it had actually happened to me. It's a very unique feeling which is challenging to put into words. When suppressed memories surface, part of you knows that they have always been there. You don't WANT to look at them, but there they are. It's almost as if someone has been standing behind you talking for a long time, but you never turned to really pay attention them before. When these memories come up, and are recognizable as the truth, they are a fuzzy yet familiar picture that has become clear for the first time. I wanted to look away and simultaneously keep looking at them because I knew they were me.

During this confusing time, I never felt so alone, but at the same time, I never felt so in touch with myself. Once this door opened, I couldn't close it. It's partly like looking in the mirror for the first time. There was no question that I was looking at myself, but it was a self that I hadn't intentionally looked at until now. It was terrifying, but also it was so real and visceral that I couldn't stop looking at it. The images of me and my father, the memories of us, were so disgusting and so real. I couldn't sweep them under the rug, just because they were disturbing. It was so obviously the truth.

That day when I was cleaning out my basement, a very specific memory of childhood sexual abuse popped up out of nowhere. As if jumping from around a corner and saying 'boo'! I put down the cardboard box I was holding, stood straight up and with an unfocused stare at the wall, I said out loud, 'no shit'. It was like opening a door and looking into a room where something is happening, but the person in the room is you. You know instantly that it's a suppressed memory and you know instantly that it's the truth.

Memory loss goes hand in hand with the confusion that it creates. I'll start by stating that the mind does not actually "lose" memories. Instead, you could say that it loses certain memories, like you might lose your keys. Your keys haven't disappeared, they haven't ceased to exist, they're simply somewhere else where you temporarily cannot find them. With instances of trauma, especially ongoing trauma, the brain will intentionally "lose" memories, temporarily putting them somewhere you cannot find them.

What I came to learn through therapy and research is that my mind was hiding vivid memories of my father sexually abusing me in order to protect me from reliving the pain of the trauma. By allowing me to "forget" the trauma, I was able to get through the experience at a young age when I was absolutely not yet equipped to deal with it. For decades, my mind continued to protect me by effectively creating a lie that the trauma never happened. When my brain disallowed me to access a memory, or multiple memories, it caused me to continually circumnavigate those parts of my past that I really should have been able to remember. Similar to driving down a highway full of dangerous obstacles, instead of being able to drive straight down the road, my brain caused me to steer right and left, forcing me to move around obstacles that could hurt me. This caused my thinking to become less linear and more erratic and confused.

My brain wasn't trying to make me suffer by doing this. On the contrary, all this zig-zagging was to protect me from pain, which is one of the brain's responsibilities. As I grew into adulthood, this ongoing circumnavigation caused a great deal of confusion and reduced my ability to concentrate effectively. Whenever I tried to think about something, I had a winding road to take if I wanted to form even simple thoughts.

In the past, brain experts looked at the brain as kind of a filing cabinet with each memory stored in its own particular drawer and folder. Today, memories are understood to be more complex in their construction, with each memory coming from many different parts of the brain at once to create a whole image or a whole memory. Thinking of something simple, like a coffee cup, requires multiple areas of the brain, not just one, to become involved simultaneously. Putting up barriers around even a single memory is very complex and is obviously limiting to normal, everyday concentration. I lived with this dysfunctional and debilitating confusion for most of my life. As I mentioned earlier, I was diagnosed with ADHD in college in the 1990s.

At the time of my attention deficit diagnosis, I was so frustrated with my reduced concentration that I actually felt relieved when I could be diagnosed with something, to explain it away. For years, I bought into what people generally told me about, "not trying hard enough", or, despite how intelligent I was, that college was turning out to be harder than I had anticipated. I started taking Ritalin, thinking it was a solution to my erratic though patterns. Like most other pharmaceuticals, it numbed me to the symptoms I was experiencing. I fell into the pharmaceutical trap of taking a pill to treat a symptom I was having, instead of looking at the problem that the symptom was trying to bring my attention to.

What was happening to me during those college years was that I was growing, evolving and working towards becoming my own man. For the first time in my life, I was outside of the old environment that was fostering my abuse (my parents, my family, my old friends, the physical places where I was sexually abused, etc). All those elements of my home environment that fostered, or allowed, my abuse were no longer around me, and I was able to finally start evolving beyond their influence.

I also chose art as a college major, which required me to think in new directions and extend my comfort zone beyond what I was raised with. I was expanding and becoming my own person for the first time in my life. I was discovering new perspectives that were in direct contradiction to the ones I had been programmed with during my upbringing. Growing up, I was taught me to be submissive and not think for myself. During these college years, I found myself caught in the middle between two opposing perspectives of life. I didn't know which filter to use when looking at the world. That dilemma, coupled with the roadblocks to my memories, created a constant and exhausting state of confusion.

This kind of internal conflict always reaches a tipping point, which in turn leads to evolution. At the time, I was incapable of understanding that a tipping point was imminent and I unknowingly shut down my process of evolving with Ritalin and other prescription ADHD drugs. This western perspective of masking any and all annoying symptoms that our bodies are experiencing so that we can "move on with our day" does not lead to healing. It is not a solution because it does not solve the problem.

When the body gives us a red flag to get our attention, like the constant confusion I was experiencing, it's asking us to look at an imbalance so we can consciously fix it. The entire reason why symptoms exist is to get our attention and to shine a light on the underlying problem that is causing the symptoms. We have to be present, aware and honest to notice and address them. In my lifetime of experience enduring all of the effects of sexual abuse, simply masking these effects with drugs is not healing. It's avoiding healing.

After about five years of taking ADHD drugs, I realized that I was stunting my healing, so I decided to stop. I knew my confusion would come back, but I felt in my heart that it was the right thing to do. When I stopped taking the drug, there was a detoxification period where I shot like a rubber band back into a state of confusion and lack of concentration. But, through that time of being able to feel my confusion, I started looking at the causes of the confusion and began to sort them out. This is when the memories of the abuse started to resurface; shocking me, scaring me and leading me down the long, dark road back to the time of the abuse. It was at this moment, standing at the precipice of everything that had been terrifying me my entire life, that my conscious journey of recovery began.

I believe that the human body is continually working to achieve optimum balance and functionality. I think the mind ultimately wants us to deal with lost memories in a way that allows us to heal from them. The brain wants to drop the barriers and road blocks it has created so it can relax into a state of balance. After all, Keeping barriers in place that block memories takes a lot of energy.

If you have experienced memory loss surrounding your abuse situation and memories are starting to resurface, my advice is to let them. Your brain is starting to smooth itself back out after hiding them from you for so long. This is the beginning of your recovery; the beginning of healing. Regaining access to your hidden memories and learning how to deal with them is progress toward finally living an enjoyable life.

Realizing and accepting my own hidden memories has made my thinking more linear because I have eradicated many of the "road blocks" my mind was using to keep me from remembering them. Ultimately the process of accepting my hidden memories has cleared up my confusion and erratic behavior. Because of this, rediscovering and dealing with lost memories has extended into and improved every aspect of my life. This is a benefit I never saw coming, but upon reflection, it makes perfect sense.

TRIGGERS

It wasn't until I had been through therapy and talked to other people who had survived abuse that I realized what a "trigger" is. Triggers are things that happen in our lives that remind us of our abuse in some way, either consciously or unconsciously. When we encounter a trigger, it causes us to have an emotional response to what is happening, even though whatever is happening may not be abuse at all. Triggers can involve interactions with other people or they can happen when we're alone. When you get "triggered", your response is typically painful, angry, or inappropriate to what is happening. Reactions to triggers are usually exaggerated and you find yourself overreacting to what is happening, either internally or externally.

I have experienced a variety of events in my life that have triggered me. Some of them are physical, like someone putting a friendly hand on me or standing too close to me. Other triggers have been verbal, like people saying things to me that remind me of what my abuser might have said to me when I was a child. The important thing to be aware of is that when someone says or does something that triggers us, most of the time they are saying or doing something friendly or even loving. They are most likely completely unaware that what they're doing is causing a painful emotional response in us.

If we are present and aware, we may notice that we're reacting to a trigger. Most of the time, however, we don't recognize it and we end up overreacting to a person or situation that does not deserve the intensified emotional response that we are offering. I know that I've been reacting to certain triggers for so many years that it's become a habit to do so. My exaggerated reactions went unnoticed and unaddressed for decades.

One example of a trigger in my life repeatedly happened when I was doing something that I would do every day, I was preparing food in my kitchen. My wife would come up behind me, put her arms around me and give me a hug. When she did this, I found myself immediately violated and angry that she had done that. My thought process was something like, "what the hell makes her think she can come into my space and put her arms around me like that without permission?". When I finally took the time to become aware of this reaction and examine it, I was initially confused because this is the woman that I love and I was getting upset by her showing affection toward me. As soon as I realized that these two sets of conflicting emotions were about the same person, I knew there was something here that was out of balance. I allowed my emotions to call my attention to a problem. When I took a moment to examine it in detail, I realized that my wife "triggered" me when she came into my personal space without permission, especially from behind. It triggered an emotional response from my past abuse, a knee-jerk reaction of violation and anger. It triggered a defense mechanism that my mind had created in response to this kind of physical contact. I may not consciously remember what exactly happened to me so many years ago to cause this specific trigger, or any trigger, but my mind certainly remembered it and wanted to defend me from it. The fact that I was having an emotional response to it is helpful because emotions are one of the indicators that our brains give us to bring our attention to an issue.

Instead of noticing it and becoming inquisitive about why I was feeling that way, I could have easily told myself that this was simply part of my personality; that I do in fact love her and want her to show affection toward me, but just not in certain ways. This is how the trigger can go unnoticed. In fact, I did ignore these triggers in other relationships throughout my life. It has only been the last few years of my life that I have been present and aware enough to notice, recognize and address these moments.

Triggers are not only confusing for the person having them, they can be equally confusing for the people on the receiving end of that anger or negative reaction. For the first couple of years in our relationship, my wife thought she was doing something "wrong" that elicited my negative responses to her loving actions. Clearly she was not. But there was no way she could have known that. What she was doing when she was showing me affection, was acting in a way that somehow reminded my mind of a physical or psychological behavior of my abuser.

In these situations, the brain will go into a defensive posture. This kind of reaction is not fair to the person who might be showing you affection, or the person talking to you at your job, or the person you don't even know who is standing in line with you at the grocery store. It takes presence, awareness and a willingness to change your behavior to identify and let these old behaviors go. Once you start noticing and addressing your reaction to triggers, the practice gains momentum, the triggers become more and more obvious and you become an automatic self-healer.

Some triggers have happened to me when I'm alone. An example of this would be when I open a cabinet and accidentally hit myself with the door. Or if I turn around in a tight space and accidentally bump into something. My reflexive response has always been to become immediately very angry. I remember in my life slamming a cabinet door shut after it bumped me, throwing something to the ground or hitting whatever bumped my head. These were clearly "fight back" responses.

Once I was present, aware and honest enough to realize that that I'm fighting back against an inanimate object, and that this action made no sense, I could begin to change my behavior. My mind was probably trying to fight back against something else that hurt me, something from my past that I was not able to fight back against at the time. I had suppressed the urge to fight back when I was a child, or maybe I was just unable to, and I was now expressing the urge to fight back as a strong adult.

When triggers bring forward an angry or defensive response, it can be fairly easy to identify. The "fight or flight" emotions seem to command our attention. Other triggers can simply make you act a certain way, like being submissive or disregarding your own safety. These are emotional responses that go more easily unnoticed.

Looking back, many triggers throughout my life made me behave in a certain way without me ever noticing. One of the most shocking of these was with my wife, early in our marriage. We were in bed and having a very loving and intimate moment, when she froze and pointed out that I was talking to her like a child. I froze, too. I got up out of bed and stood there for a moment realizing that she was right. I had been talking like a little boy without even noticing it. The intimate sexual contact between my wife and I had brought up something from my past that made me talk that way. It was so shocking and nauseating to me that I went into the bathroom to vomit. Although it was sickening, this was a powerful moment of realization which ultimately helped me move forward in my recovery. This experience helped me take back the power to realize what I was doing, what I was saying and what I was thinking.

The way to deal with behavioral triggers is to notice them without judgement. Be present, be aware, stop what you are doing and take a moment to shine a light on what's happening. If I'm alone, I stop what I'm doing and typically talk it out either in my head or aloud. If I'm with my wife or a friend, I'll stop and talk it out with them. People who are close to me, who care about me always understand what's going on after I explain it, and I'm usually congratulated on having another breakthrough.

Identifying one of your own personal triggers is a great moment of empowerment. You can then redefine your reaction to the triggering event, or you can simply let it go. As someone once told me, a habit is only a habit until you become aware of it — then it becomes a choice. It may take a while to change your habit, because you may have had a lifetime of reacting to certain events in certain ways, but once you realize it, then you are in control. Be patient as you retrain yourself. Eventually, you will get to decide how you want to react when someone who loves you comes up and surprises you with a hug. Get some momentum going with noticing your triggers and make it a new practice. Go through the motions of stopping what you're doing, give that person a hug back and decide that you are in control of your reactions — not your abuser.

SHAME AND BLAME

Two of the biggest side effects of sexual abuse are laying blame on ourselves for what happened, then, in turn, carrying around enormous amounts of shame for it. Although we may not initially realize it, pointing accusatory feelings at ourselves is misguided. People can spend a lifetime feeling responsible for their own abuse and trying to redirect these heavy feelings of shame and blame.

When people look back on their abuse, they seem to involuntarily say, "How could I have let that happen?". This kind of thinking is unfair. Throughout our entire lives, we're always doing the best we can with the existing skills we have at the time. As a young child, I had no skills to deal with what was happening around me or to me. My father took advantage of this when he abused me. Now, as an adult who has spent time in therapy and who has done my own work to attain the skills to look at abuse situations in an empowering way, the situation is completely different. If someone were to try and manipulate or abuse me today, like my father did so many years ago, I would easily be able to recognize it and stop it. However, when my memories first started coming back, and I realized I was abused, I did what most people unfortunately do. I unconsciously looked back at my younger self through the eyes of someone who has my current adult skill set. I judged myself from my current perspective for not being able to see what was happening to stop the abuse. In doing so, my conclusion was to blame myself for what happened.

When it comes to shame and blame, what I learned through therapy is that I didn't "let" my abuser do anything to me. He was in a position of complete power over me, not only physically because he was so much bigger than me, but psychologically because he was both an adult as well as my father. It was his duty as my father to protect me. Instead, he attacked me. It was his duty as my father to raise me up and help me to become strong. Instead, he suppressed me and made me feel weak. As a child, with a child's skill set, I knew no different. I didn't do anything, nor could I have done anything, that warranted any kind of blame. Also, when I factored-in the environment in which the abuse happened, I found other elements, in addition to my abuser himself, that disempowered me even more.

One of these environmental elements was what I was

being taught at public school. My teachers told me to listen to my parents and do whatever they told me to do. So, not only was I not able to see that I was being abused, much less being able to do anything about it, but I was being programmed at school to live with whatever was going on at home. As a child, I had no chance of realizing or stopping what was happening to me at home. The more I took the time to look at my childhood abuse situation from my adult perspective and digest it, the more I realized that self blame made no sense at all.

Whatever your abuse situation was, it was another person doing something to you that you did not want. Just because you did not have the ability to stop it at the time, doesn't mean that you asked for it, condoned it, or are responsible for it happening. Self-blame and the associated shame are not your burdens to carry!

Shame for me was not only caused by my self blame, it also came from wanting to spend time with my father, even though he was my abuser. We all want and need love, especially as children. As a child, I expected to get love from my parents. When "love" came in the form of sexual contact, I thought that's what love was. My father made me feel special through this attention. One of the ways that child molesters can get away with what they are doing is by teaching the children that the sexual contact is happening because they "love the child so much". Regardless of whether he made me feel special or loved, what he did to me was absolutely wrong. It's up to parents to make their children feel loved without sexual contact.

The fact that I wanted to spend time with my father, to get the attention I so desperately needed as a child, was absolutely not an indication that I wanted to have sexual contact with him. I needed real love and safe, non-abusive attention. (I discuss the definition of love in chapter eight.) I see this now and I no longer feel shame for wanting to spend time with my father, even taking into account what that man did to me.

Another reason for holding onto shame can be a feeling of enjoyment that the victim may have received from the abuse. The sexual acts that an abuser performs on his victim, depending on what they are, can be physically stimulating and cause the body to react in a pleasurable way. This can be very confusing, especially for a child. If a survivor of sexual abuse recalls even a fractional memory of "enjoying" the sexual experience, it can create a lifetime of shame. Survivors can confusingly and wrongly believe that they "enjoyed being violated". To resolve this, it is important to spend time unpacking the memories of the situation and examining what happened.

Regarding childhood sexual abuse, a confused, young child who is a victim of unsolicited sexual contact is being introduced to these things prematurely for the first time, and is in no way prepared to understand what is happening. He or she may physically enjoy what is happening even though it is a violation. The abused child has no context with which to compare these new experiences and is not deserving of either blame nor shame. The only ability children have, when they come into the world, is to completely trust those adults around them to treat them with respect and care. They are completely vulnerable targets for adults who have sinister intentions.

Abuse situations happen when one person trusts another person who has power over them. When the person in power abuses their position and breaks that trust, that's the beginning of abuse. If you were abused, you were not in power and you were not in control. There is no reason for you to blame yourself or have any shame surrounding your abuse.

If you're still wrestling with self-blame or shame, my

advice is to get professional help with these incredibly debilitating, disempowering and often confusing feelings. A therapist can help you sort out and redirect these feelings which will empower you to move forward with a new, healthy perspective.

LOW SELF ESTEEM

Seeing yourself as not being worthy of anything is a very common perspective after an abuse situation. The root cause of my reduced self worth came from not understanding WHY my father was doing what he was doing to me. He abused me when I was a very young boy and he certainly didn't explain to me the truth about why he was doing what he was doing. He performed sexual acts with me and then left me to figure out why it was happening for myself. At that age and at that level of understanding, I did not yet have the ability to understand the wrongness of the situation, nor could I understand my father's motivations. He was teaching me that this was my role in life, that this was my place in the world, that this was who I was. He taught me that I was his toy to do with as he wanted, that I was less than human and that what I wanted – or did not want – did not matter. I was not being given a fundamental level of human respect at this early age in my life.

My father did such an effective job of teaching me that I was not worthy of anything, that I carried that perspective into my behavior for the next thirty years of my life. Looking back, I can see my behavior that showed this. I was constantly asking for other people's opinions about what I was doing, instead of deciding myself that it was good enough. I had low self esteem through school, during my time in the army, and throughout my college years. I never asked myself what I wanted. I was always asking someone else. I would also "settle" for things instead of working for something better. I would take a job that paid a certain minimal amount, but not more. I would receive something that I bought online or ordered at a restaurant, only to find out it was not what I ordered, and I would settle for it. I never strived for more.

The tools to solve low self esteem are presence and awareness. They allow you to pause, see what's happening and recognize it. I still catch myself, today, acting like my opinion doesn't matter and that I don't deserve things. It's rare, but it still occasionally happens. The difference is that now, I'm aware of it, and that makes all the difference. I can now catch myself in moments of acting with low self esteem or that my opinion does not matter and I immediately counter-act it. I now realize that I am a human being and not someone's play thing. And, with that status of being a human being, I get to have my own desires, I get to make my own decisions, and I'm deserving of whatever I want.

SUBMISSIVENESS

My submissive behavior, which I can now look back and easily recognize, went hand-in-hand with my lack of self worth. I entered into every situation of my life like an employee, rather than a boss. I felt like my opinion couldn't mean anything because I, myself, didn't mean anything. Without my opinion meaning anything, I would submit to everyone else's opinions. I was a passive, unconscious player in my own life for decades.

As I grew older, I unconsciously sought out and attached myself to abusive men who I made subconsciously into surrogate father figures. I did this because being abused and controlled felt like home to me. I chose to feel this way about several of my bosses, one of my drill sergeants in basic training and other people in my life who were older than me and with whom I could feel comfortable playing a submissive role. Realizing this behavior and shining a light on it was a powerful step to putting an end to yet another bad habit.

Most survivors of childhood sexual abuse have relationship problems as adults. Abused children are taught to be submissive to abuser's desires, then that behavior is unconsciously carried into adulthood. Then, as adults, abuse survivors put other people's needs and desires above their own. Abusees inherently want to habitually please everyone else, without even thinking about it. We also do it under the guise of being chivalrous, kind or wonderfully selfless. But if we look at our behavior with present awareness, we will also probably see that we lack assertiveness, we don't hold value in our own opinions and we lack the ability to set boundaries in all of our relationships. This has been an empowering realization for me on my own recovery journey. I found immense freedom by noticing these traits and, one by one, letting them go.

This technique is something you can experiment with. It's always empowering and actually fun to do. Let's play with this right now. As you're reading this, pause and think of a relationship that you have; either a family member, a friend or a work colleague. Think about a behavior of theirs that you find hurtful. Decide right now that you're going to set a new boundary for yourself and that you won't put up with it anymore. For example, decide right now that you're going to say something about it the next time you're with them, when they are doing that hurtful thing. Think about what you're going to say to them; play it out in your head a few times in a few different ways. It's important to speak your mind in a way that is specifically NOT angry. It can be as simple as saying, "Hey, what you just said was really hurtful. Would you please not say that anymore?" It just has to come from your heart. If it comes from your heart, you won't have to memorize what you're going to say, it will just come out of you naturally. Know that it won't play out exactly as you've imagined. But the important thing is to embrace your new perspective, embrace your new boundary and be ready for the next time that it happens.

I went through this process with an old army buddy of mine who was visiting from out of town. He came over to our home for a drink with me and my wife. When we were in the army together, his twenty-year-old self always joked around by calling me a "loser". It was a signature comment of his, not only for me, but for everyone else as well. Sure enough, when he was visiting us, twenty years later, I was in the middle of telling him a story and he laughed and called me a loser. It made me very uncomfortable. I let his comment hang in the air without an immediate response and I looked at my wife, who looked appalled. Then I finally said, "You know what, you're going to have to stop calling me a loser". He said he was just joking and that he didn't mean it. So I replied, "If you don't mean it, then don't say it". The discussion about the word loser went on for a couple more minutes and ultimately I told him that I don't let anyone talk to me like that anymore, and I would appreciate it if he would stop saying that to me. I wasn't angry, I was confident and it made me feel empowered.

Since that day, which is now years ago, he hasn't even reached out to me to say hi or ask how I'm doing. Setting boundaries and standing up for yourself also acts like a filter for people. Those who actually care about you will appreciate your spoken boundaries and support the fact that you're growing and learning to take care of yourself. People who don't understand, will bounce off of you and go their own way. My advice is not to lament one unfit friendship. There are billions of people in the world. Make some new friends who do care about you, who don't speak with abuse disguised as humor, and with whom you don't need to be submissive.

ADDICTIVE BEHAVIOR

People exhibiting addictive behavior are usually distracting themselves from the problems that they don't want to deal with. Whether it's drugs, alcohol, video games or anything else, when people relentlessly engage in something that has no purpose other than distraction, it's time for them to take a closer look at it. Maybe the activity their engaging in no longer has a place in their life, at least not at the frequency at which they do it. For years, I let several things become addictive for me until I finally realized these behaviors were keeping me distracted and keeping me from healing.

My addictive behavior became obvious to me at the beginning of my journey in healing. After my first therapist helped me remember enough about my abuse that I was sure it happened, I stopped my therapy to give myself time to digest this new information. Instead of digesting it so I could move forward in a positive way, I unconsciously went the other direction. I went into hiding. I started a relationship with a woman who was also sexually abused as a child for several years. I saw that she wasn't dealing with her issues, so I decided to follow her lead and not deal with mine either. Our relationship lasted nine years. During that time, I completely avoided dealing with the effects of my abuse while my life quietly became a downward spiral. At the end of that relationship, at the deepest point of my depression, I was exhibiting several extreme addictive behaviors.

I had thrown myself into an underpaying job that I hated and spent long hours at work. It was an extremely demanding career that kept me busy all the time, even when I was not physically at work. Even though there were low self esteem factors that caused me to take this job for such low pay, it's obvious, in retrospect, that my job became an addiction.

I was a member at a local health club where I exercised three times a day; before work, during lunch, and after work before I went home. When I told my doctor at my annual physical that I was lifting weights and doing cardio four hours a day, six days a week, he asked me if I was a professional athlete, because those are the only people who work out that much. I said no, that I worked sitting in an office all day. He still mentioned that I should look at how much I was going to the gym.

Also, during all of this, I was drinking so much that it honestly should have killed me. I was buying vodka by the case and drinking myself into a drunken sleep every night. Additionally, I would power-drink coffee from the moment I got up, until happy hour in the afternoon. I had several other addictive habits that were legal and that went unnoticed by myself and everyone else. They included playing video games, watching movies, and other non-productive pastimes. These were all "normal" things to do, but I was participating in them at a level that was designed to either keep me away from my problems or keep me away from home and the woman who represented my problems because she was an abuse survivor as well.

In retrospect, I can see why I was overloading myself with all those addictive behaviors. It's obvious to me now that I was working very hard to distract myself from dealing with the memories of the abuse that would not go away. At the time, however, I was so far inside of my situation that I was completely blind to it. Nobody who looked at me from the outside could tell that I was doing any of these things in excess. Ultimately I had to recognize it for myself so that I could change it.

Spotting addictive behavior in yourself takes presence, awareness and honesty. The combination of these three tools takes practice but, like anything else, it gets easier the more you do it. The key is to take a moment right when you're in the middle of doing something that you enjoy doing and ask yourself, "why am I doing this? No, really… why am I doing this?". The activity that you are questioning is usually something that you think you're enjoying. For example, I really thought I enjoyed drinking, and at one point I may have, but I was drinking in excess and I wasn't looking at why I was doing it. At one point I probably really enjoyed working out at the gym, but again I was exercising beyond rational limits. The long hours I spent at a job that I didn't enjoy, should have been a red flag - and it eventually was.

The answer you give yourself when you question your behavior in these situations has to be honest. Don't hide anything from yourself. Trust yourself. Care about yourself. Call yourself out on your own destructive behavior. Then, instead of blaming yourself for it, just change it.

When the distraction of addictive behavior doesn't work to keep a person's mind away from what is bringing them pain, people sometimes end up hurting or killing themselves. I consider myself lucky that suicide is not in my nature. I have known people who have killed themselves during times of depression, but I thankfully never related to that as a viable course of action. My reaction to massive depression was that if things really got too bad in my life, I would just walk away and start completely over somewhere else. I eventually hit a tipping point and did exactly that. I hit the reset button on my life.

I remember the day it happened very clearly. I had flown out to the east coast with my ex to visit her parents for a week during the holidays. I have always been an early-riser, so I got up before everyone that first morning and went downstairs in their very nice house to make coffee. On my way through the living room to the kitchen, something stopped me in my tracks. I turned around, looking at everything in that very nice house and said to myself, "I'm done here. I'm done with all of this." I think I even said it out loud. It was my intuition talking to me and I was listening. It was a quiet morning, I was alone and I was on vacation in a place where I had to leave my addictions behind for a few days. I was away from my job, my gym, my video games, my movies and everything else I depended on to take my mind off of my problems. When I began to relax, it felt like my higher self spoke to me and I was apparently calm enough and undistracted enough to hear it.

When I got back home from that trip, a fire had grown in my belly that I had never felt before. I quit my job, quit my gym membership and ended my unhealthy relationship. Shortly after that, I quit drinking alcohol. Eventually, I quit drinking coffee, as well. It was a huge set of changes over a few short months and it was also a huge waypoint in my journey of recovery. I started doing research on things that would help me heal from the effects. I set new boundaries and kept them. When I did all this, the universe responded by putting someone in my life who gave me true love and support. It gave me the woman who was to become my wife.

COMFORT EATING

One of my symptoms that went unnoticed for a long time was that I ate food to comfort myself. When I say it like that, it sounds pretty normal. Being hungry is uncomfortable, so eating relieves that. But the eating that I'm talking about is an unconscious habit that comes from depression. The comfort eating that I was experiencing deserves separate attention from other addictive behaviors because I wasn't excessively eating to simply distract myself from dealing with my past. I was eating specifically to find emotional comfort. In the absence of real love from my parents, I turned to other things to feel a sense of love, or to feel comforted. I turned to food, not when I was genuinely hungry, but when I was upset or feeling empty of love.

Food is something that was always there, it was always satisfying and it never failed to "fill me up" when I was feeling empty or lonely. So many people create an unhealthy relationship with food because of these pleasing factors. It took me a long time to realize that food is not a human friend who cares about me. Food is not a passionate lover or a caring parent. Food cannot replace a thoughtful person who may not exist in my life. Food is simply the fuel that we put into our bodies to stay alive. Human society has built an enormous culture around food, which I think can be wonderful in its diversity and playfulness. Enjoying the fuel we put into our bodies and turning it into an art form is cool. But using food to try to fill a hole in your heart will not work.

Treating food like an antidepressant can not only be unhealthy for your body, it's a practice of turning to something that cannot solve the problem. Whether it's food, drugs, alcohol, or any other addictive behavior, these things you might turn to can only make you feel good for a short time. They all have the potential to turn into a constant practice that a person can never, ever get enough of. In retrospect, I was personally eating to replace the missing love in my life. I finally realized that food doesn't work that way.

If you think you eat in excess of your physical hunger for one of these reasons, take an honest look at yourself. At the moment you decide to get something to eat, especially if it's just a snack, be present and take an honest look at WHY you're deciding to eat at that moment. If you're truly hungry, then great, go get something to eat. But if not, ask yourself if you are turning to eating because of a negative emotion, and empty feeling, or loneliness. If this is the case then, after you eat something, ask yourself if you become depressed or unfulfilled like before you ate. It might be time to create a healthy relationship with food instead of using it to try and treat a negative emotional state.

If you'd like help in exploring what a healthy relationship with food is, a therapist can definitely work with you to see things clearly. It's a very common topic that is well researched and discussed in therapy. If you're not ready to go into therapy for what might be comfort eating, I would suggest starting your exploration by using presence and awareness to pay attention to when you're eating and why you're doing it.

MAKING BAD FRIENDS

Business success gurus tell us that our individual personality is the culmination of the half-dozen or so people we choose to spend the most time with. I've always thought this was true, especially when I look at the people I've always chosen to spend my time with. I also grew up hearing that "birds of a feather flock together", which I also thought to be a valid axiom.

As I moved through therapy and became more analytical, I looked at these two philosophies and realized a big difference. The first one is an active statement, saying that you CHOOSE to hang around with certain people. The second statement is passive, suggesting that you spend time with others unconsciously. I think I've lived most of my life following the second, passive philosophy.

Looking back on when I was exhibiting so many negative behaviors based on the effects of my abuse, I would unconsciously spend my time with anyone who simply allowed me to spend time with them. Whether through low self esteem, submissiveness, or wanting to please others over myself, I ended up with people who were as damaged as I was, or who enabled my negative behavior. Some of them were very submissive, like me, while others were controlling and abusive. It's these negative people who, in addition to my parents, had a huge influence on my forming personality as I was growing up. By osmosis and through association, I allowed these negative people to teach me how to think, feel and act about the world, and what prejudices or perspectives to hold onto.

As I became and adult, I just kept following the same methodology. I passively flocked together with other birds of my feather and unconsciously spent time with the same kinds of negative people. I surrounded myself with people who liked to commiserate, rather than solve any of their own problems, who were abusive to me or who were controlling. It wasn't until the last decade of my life that I have become an active chooser of the people I decide to spend time with.

With this new empowering perspective, I started really looking at my current adult relationships, and started to make some major changes. I decided to set some new boundaries on who I let become close to me, and who I let into my life at all. I sat down in front of my computer and, in about half an hour, I chopped my social media friends from hundreds down to about seventy. I also stopped going out and spending time with most of my so-called friends. I even eventually stopped talking to most of my family, which was a radical diversion from the way I behaved my entire life. When I made these huge changes, I thought that anyone who was truly my friend or who truly cared about me would respond to me by phone or email. I thought they would want to ask me why I stopped talking to them, or why I "un-friended" them online. Out of all those hundreds of people that I suddenly cut out of my life, a total of two reached back out to me to find out why they hadn't heard from me. Both of those people came back at me with anger, rather than curiosity, and neither of those people were members of my family. This was surprising, truly satisfying, empowering and I was happy with the result. Clearly I had removed people from my life who didn't really care about me, at least not in the way that I wanted to be cared about.

Moving forward, I decided to start choosing who I spent my precious time with. Those new people I met who didn't know how to speak to me with respect were not allowed access to me. I simply turned and went my own way. Taking back the power of my decision and my preference made me feel strong and confident.

These were all bold moves and it was initially a little bit frightening, but I have to admit that it was exciting, as well. A deep part of me knew that I needed to get these people out of my life. It felt like taking off a heavy, old coat that didn't fit me anymore. In fact, it never did. Someone simly told me to put on that old, heavy coat and, at some point in my upbringing, I did. My whole life, I was just putting up with it. Ultimately, it was my lack of self worth that made me reach out to anyone and everyone who would have me as a friend, instead of being discriminatory based on what was best for me. These days, I have far fewer friends, but the friends I do have accept me for who I am, and care deeply about me as I do about them. I would not trade one of them for a hundred of the others.

If you take a look at the relationships in your life, I bet you will realize that some of them, or possibly most of them, are negative, abusive or in some way just not good for you. My advice is to consider ending these relationships that aren't mutually supportive, that aren't mutually caring and that ultimately lower your personal energy level - your frequency. As I've said before, there are billions of people in the world to choose from. Decide intentionally to find new relationships with people who help you to raise your standards and with whom you can equally exchange your energy.

NOTICING NEGATIVE BELIEF SYSTEMS

As we grow up, we are injected with the belief systems of the people who raised us. It's typically an involuntary process and we're unaware of it as it's happening. These people actually give us our first perspectives of the world around us, as well as our perspectives of who we are. It usually isn't until we move out of our parents' house that we have the opportunity to start challenging those belief systems and maybe even creating some of our own. So many people, especially adults with abusive pasts, never challenge these hand-me-down beliefs and instead just keep thinking, talking and acting like their parents. I was absolutely one of these people.

At seventeen years old, I left home and went into the world operating on a set of mixed perspectives from my parents, from other adults in my life, and from the friends I was spending time with while I was growing up. Most, if not all, of these people did not hold my personal well-being as a priority, nor their own personal well-being for that matter. In retrospect, these belief systems and perspectives were less than what I would consider self-empowering. I carried these self-destructive beliefs all the way into my middle-age years and I was not consciously aware of them. I held onto them because I didn't know how to see them or how to change them. I didn't even know I had the ability to change them.

For example, I remember my father as a racist and a homophobe when I was growing up. He would let bigoted remarks fly across the dinner table or in other conversations around our home. He would not make these comments in public, so, by his example, I was taught how to quietly hate other people, to take traits from other people who were different from me and use them as a reason to quietly belittle them. Looking back, my father had very low self esteem. It takes someone with low self worth as a foundation to their personality to use a bigoted perspective. They try to boost themselves up by tearing other people down.

Additionally, a lot of these negative belief systems I was living with were reinforcing the negative behaviors I was already exhibiting because of the abuse. Beliefs like, "I'm not worthy of great things" or "my opinions aren't important", or "I'll just settle for and accept what other people tell me about myself." I needed to let go of the negative belief systems that other people had put into my head. Then, I needed to create some of my own that would allow me to grow in a healthy way. All in all, I had a lot of work to do in order to grow into a loving, balanced human being.

There were two things that helped me to see my negative belief systems. The first one was therapy. Therapists are trained to shine a light into the dark corners of your mind. Then they ask bold questions which makes you give them bold answers. When you answer them honestly, you actually start to speak these hand-me-down belief systems out loud before you realize it. When you do this, an awesome thing happens. The belief systems coming out of your mouth start to obviously contradict the person that you are and you begin to actually see what's going on inside you. This realization is a beautiful and empowering moment, kind of like watching an amazing sunrise. It can be simultaneously wonderful and overwhelming.

These negative belief systems are bad habits. Worse than that, they are somebody else's bad habits that you have taken on as your own. Don't judge yourself or blame yourself for holding onto them, simply let them go as you identify them. Again, once you become aware of a habit, it's no longer a habit. It becomes a choice. Once you see one of these negative belief systems operating inside of you, for the rest of your life you'll always be able to see it. It will never be able to hide again. When you see it and you don't like it, you can let it go. If it tries to pop up again, it will be a very obvious and unwanted guest. You can simply re-escort it to the door and show it the way out.

The second thing that helped me see my belief systems was my own research into the topic. Eckhart Tolle's book, *The Power of Now*, helped me to very simply break apart my thought processes. Once you can look at your thoughts as they are disassembled, you can clearly see the belief systems that don't serve you. Another great source for helping to notice negative belief systems are the messages of Bashar, channeled by Daryl Anka. Bashar talks about negative belief systems as somebody else's luggage that you're literally carrying around with you until you decide to put them down, allowing yourself to feel lighter.

Once I noticed that these negative belief systems were operating inside me, it was Buddhism and meditation that helped me to let go of them so that I could create some new ones for myself. I discuss meditation in Chapter 7, but I wanted to mention it here just to say that it IS possible to permanently change they way that we have been thinking our entire lives. In fact, I've done it and I've watched other people do it. It's the most empowering thing I've ever experienced in myself and the most exciting thing I've ever watched anybody else go through.

DEFINING LOVE DURING ABUSE

At a time when young children are learning about the world around them for the first time, an abuser can skew a child's definitions about everything. When that abuser is someone who is supposed to be taking care of that child, like a parent, he or she definitely gives the child a skewed perspective on the concept of love.

One of the things I unconsciously learned from my parents and friends while I was growing up was a dark, heavy, negative definition of love. Before I had a chance to learn what love was on my own, or to be taught a healthy definition of love from someone who had my best interests in mind, I had my abuser's definition of love forced upon me.

My father taught me that love means hurting the people you are supposed to be taking care of. My mother taught me that love means not paying attention to the people who are close to you. My bad friends at the time taught me that love meant getting what you can out of a relationship, not caring about what the other person needs or thinks, having sex without emotional content and disregarding commitment. I unconsciously carried pieces of all of these definitions with me into my adult life without realizing or addressing any of them.

Of course, all of these negative definitions of love that I was holding onto caused me and other people pain throughout my life. These definitions created challenging situations every time I got into a relationship with anyone, whether it was with lovers or friends. When a person is unaware that he or she is holding onto other people's definitions, instead of creating their own, they don't understand why they have unhappiness in their lives. They don't understand that these involuntarily-acquired definitions are in contradiction to who they are. That struggle causes a constant, low-level, background pain which flares up occasionally, but is always there. When people don't know how to notice these negative definitions, they just go on living with the pain, thinking that love must be pain. I go into detail about redefining love in Chapter 8, but I wanted to mention negative definitions of love here as a definite and direct effect of the abuse and of the environment surrounding the abuse.

In retrospect, whenever I would get into a relationship in my life, I saw the same formulaic behavior repeatedly play out. I would excitedly rush into the relationship at 100mph because I was so in need of love. I wanted to be in a loving relationship more than anything. Then, when the relationship would become more serious, that person would become someone I would have to start trusting. I would then immediately start to not trust them because my unconscious definition of love was that the person who loves me would hurt me. I would then emotionally push them away and keep my distance from them. My relationship partner would be very confused and, actually, so would I.

My definition of love was so buried, and interwoven with my definition of myself, that I couldn't see it. I was unaware that I was sabotaging myself by holding onto the definition of love that my father and others taught me. Each relationship would inevitably end and I would move onto another one, thinking that last person must not have been the right one for me. It wasn't until much later in my recovery journey that I was able to see this negative definition of love and let it go.

CYNICISM

Cynicism is defined as "an inclination to believe that people are motivated by self-interest". As someone who experienced my father taking complete advantage of me when I was three years old, it's easy to see how I was taught to be cynical. But my cynicism didn't only come from my father. It also came from my mother, who was psychologically abused by my father. She was also eventually abandoned by my him, which helped to teach her to be cynical, as well. He was the only serious relationship my mother ever had in her entire life, and he walked away from our family to start another family with another woman. After my father left, I had my mother's cynical attitude toward life and love as an example until I moved out to go to college. I don't blame her for holding onto that cynicism because it was a defense mechanism. She was doing the best she could in that situation with what she had been taught. I now look back and recognize these two people as the ones who taught me their perspectives on being self-interested. I absorbed these belief systems and, again, unconsciously carried them into my adult life.

For me to realize and recognize this cynical perspective in myself, it had to be pointed out to me by someone who loves me dearly, my wife. I'm inspired by my wife for so many incredible reasons, one of which is that she is constantly motivated by a perspective of self-empowerment. Early in our relationship, I recognized and respected her perspective on the world, but simultaneously thought it was not for me. Ultimately, this was because it clashed with the cynical belief system that my parents taught me. Because I learned and created my new habit of analyzing my own behavior, I was able to recognize my underlying cynicism during a simple event that happened in my life that most people may not think twice about.

It was a seemingly mundane but poignant moment in our kitchen that pivoted my awareness of my cynicism. One of our kitchen appliances was a three-year-old blender which had a broken lid that kept us from using it. It was a very nice and expensive blender and we didn't want to have to buy a new one just because the lid was broken, so my wife suggested that we call the company and order a new lid. My immediate reaction was that the blender company would tell us to go to the store and buy a whole new blender because they don't replace just the lid. I stood there doing the dishes and my wife called the company on speaker phone so I could hear it. It sounded like they did actually replace parts on their blenders, like the lid, and they started asking her questions about proof of purchase and how long we had owned the blender. Since we had owned it for three years, and I knew the standard one year warranty had expired, it was obvious to me that the lid could not possibly be under warranty. Again, my cynical perspective was that she would have to order a new lid and it would be wildly overpriced. Then, she would have to pay for shipping which would, again, be more expensive than it should be.

After talking with the company representative for about five minutes, he said they would not only send us a new lid, but they would not charge us for it. He also said they would pay for three-day shipping, as well. I was dumbfounded. I stopped doing the dishes and stood there for a moment, staring at her with my mouth hanging open. This is when my awareness kicked in. I immediately became aware of how negative my attitude was toward not only that situation, but other situations and about life in general. This awareness of my acquired cynical belief system gave me the power to let it go because it didn't fit who I wanted to be. But I would not have been able to let it go if I had not first become aware of it. Practicing awareness of your own behavior and being honest about what you see is the key to recognizing acquired belief systems that are not serving you.

VICTIM MENTALITY

Someone once said, "there are two ways to look at the world. The first is 'wow, look at all this stuff that's happening'. The second is 'wow, look at all this stuff that's happening TO ME'. In the second statement, you are painting yourself as a victim." It was my father who literally made me a victim. He showed me physically and emotionally what it is like to be a victim. Additionally, my mother taught me about how to hold onto the victim mentality and make it part of my life. The victim mentality is a passive way to see life and it is disempowering.

Looking back to before I intentionally started to heal, I can see the victim mentality in almost all of the people I chose to spend time with, so it's no surprise that I unconsciously acquired that perspective. If I encountered someone who was a proactive person, who didn't see themselves as a victim in life, I simply couldn't relate to them, so I didn't spend time with them. I actually found them unconsciously threatening. Now that I can spot the victim mentality, I notice it almost everywhere today. I encounter it when I talk to people I meet in business and in my personal life. I hear it in the language used by people in public when I listen to them talking as I pass by. It's sad to me how prevalent it is in our society. The most important element here is that I heard it in the language that I myself was using. This awareness allowed me to take that next step and change it. I didn't learn how to make changes in myself from my parents. I learned that on my own and you can, too.

These days, I pay close attention to the words I choose when I'm speaking with people. I will actually stop in the middle of a sentence and say, "let me rephrase that…" and I'll start again, saying it in a way that empowers me and takes me out of the victim mentality. An example of this is I might say something like, "Let me get that for you". Then I will become aware of it and change it to something like, "I'm going to get that for you". The second statement takes me away from sounding like I'm asking permission and puts me into a position of making a decision and declaring it.

I also choose to spend my time with people who are proactive about their lives and are aware of how they speak as well. When I decided to let go of my old 'friends' who mostly saw themselves as victims, I found it was about 99% of the people I was choosing to spend time with. Like I said previously, I just stopped talking to them and almost all of them didn't seem to notice or were too submissive to respond to me. I simply never heard from them again. I sought out new friends and new business associates who were not in the victim mentality either.

After I became aware of the victim mentality perspective, I spent decades trying to raise my mother up out of her victim mentality. Sadly, I learned that you can't change someone else, especially if they don't want to change. My mother could not let go of her negative perspective of how the world only exists to beat her down so, eventually, for my own progress on my journey, I let her go, too.

BROKEN TRUST

When we are born into this world, we depend on people to take care of us. We are in a position of having to trust our parents or guardians completely. We trust them to teach us how to eat, walk, talk, and look at the world around us. In my case, my father broke this trust. Instead of focusing on taking care of me, my father used me to take care of himself. I was taught right from the beginning that, when I trust someone, I get hurt. He handed me a belief system that told me trust is foolish. Trusting someone is a natural way to be. Not trusting anyone is something you have to be taught. Clearly my father believed this himself because he was taught this from someone else in his life, probably his parents. From what my father taught me at that early age, I learned not to trust any other adult in my life, including my mother. It was clear to me, when I was a child, that all these big adults around me could not be trusted to take care of me. I learned that I had to take care of myself, to watch my own back, and to trust absolutely no one. In that sense, from the age of three years old, I became a premature adult.

Now that I'm in my 50's, I realize that, because I blamed myself for allowing the abuse to happen, I couldn't even trust myself to take care of myself. Which made me a dysfunctional premature adult. I carried this lack of trust very quietly into my adult life and it seeped into everything I said and did. As I grew up, I never really trusted anyone and, sadly, I never really trusted myself. This was an enormous foundational paradigm that colored everything I was thinking during the first forty years of my life. Looking back, I can see now that I would even make myself promises and then unconsciously not keep them to reinforce this paradigm. Promises meant nothing to me and trust was a lie.

As I look at the cycle of broken trust in the generations of my family, and other people's families, I become aware of it. Once I become aware of it, I can choose to do something about it. I can choose to change the way I think about trust.

CONTROL

As I grew into an adult, I felt like I needed to have control over everything in my life. This may not sound abnormal when you state it like that, but the need to have control over everything is not healthy. Today, it's easy for me to see that trying to control everything that's happening around me in the world all of the time is simply impossible. However, because I didn't have control when I was being abused as a child, I wanted to exercise control over everything as an adult to feel safe. Because I can't control everything that happens in my life, this desire would constantly fail and cause me to feel frustration and pain.

Throughout my life, as in anyone's life, there were countless examples of situations that I attempted to control, but the most obvious one was the need to control intimate interactions. My wife pointed out that almost every time we're pausing during our day to give each other a long hug, or when we're lying in bed, wrapped around each other in the morning, I would always say something like, "I have to get up and do something, but I'll hug you for just another minute". This was me exhibiting control over the intimate situation because, now as an adult, I have the power to do so. For her, relaxing and being vulnerable in a moment of intimacy was what she enjoyed about that hug moment. For me, I could not be vulnerable. I could not relax until I had control over the situation. Her perception of it was that I thought doing something else was more important than being near her, or that I wanted to leave because I wasn't enjoying that intimate moment. For me, I unconsciously needed that control to be able to even come close to relaxing. It took me years to figure out this dynamic situation on my own. But now that I'm aware of it, I can work to relax into the moment and realize that this person is trying to express love and not trying to control me or hurt me.

To identify control issues in yourself, be honest with yourself and notice what's happening. If someone else, like the person you might be in a relationship with, points out that you're behaving in a similar way, don't let anger take over and discount what they are saying. Anger can come up because what they are saying is threatening your control of the situation. Take a moment, take a breath and consider what they are saying. Be aware of what you're doing. It's probably a key to another belief system you can change in yourself for the better.

ANGER, HATE AND FRUSTRATION

For decades after my abuse, I felt an enormous amount of anger. It was mostly directed at my father, but it soon became clear that there was more anger than I originally noticed. Through therapy, I realized that I also felt anger at my mother for not doing anything to stop the abuse. There was also a quieter, deeper anger toward every other adult that was around me at that time for not noticing what was going on and helping me. And finally, I felt anger at myself because I thought I should have been able to somehow stop the abuse. Carrying around this much unresolvable anger ultimately led to profound frustration, which made me feel helpless.

Once you let anger move into your heart, it dominates. When you become used to being angry at your abuser all the time, that practice carries over into having anger as a reaction to almost every other challenging person or situation in your life. Anger spreads inside of you like a wildfire. You become angry at coworkers for little things, you become angry at the cashier at the grocery store, and you become angry at the person driving in front of you on the road. Anger becomes the go-to response in practically everything you do. It controls your thoughts, your actions and the decisions that you make which take your life into new directions.

Society teaches us, through the news, Hollywood movies, TV shows, books and video games that hate is a totally justified emotion when someone hurts us. But, they go farther than that, they make anger look cool. Like so many other people, I bought into that perspective when I was growing up. I started looking up to angry and violent men who appeared to be so strong. We've all seen movies and read books where one of the "hero's" loved ones is either hurt or killed by the "bad guy". Our hero then spends the entire story "getting back" at the bad guy, usually by killing him. These stories usually don't focus on the hero's emotional state after he achieves his revenge. Typically the movie or story just ends. We are even taught to call it a "happy ending" because he achieved his hateful revenge on the person who hurt him.

With these messages being pumped into us from all directions, it may even feel "wrong" to let go of your anger. It's not easy to call something a "problem" when it's so obviously supported by society. It's very important to realize, however, that anger IS a problem. We're taught that anger is a form of strength, or that if you use your anger "correctly", you can draw strength from it, but that's the opposite of the truth. Anger is a raging fire that just keeps growing, using your energy as the fuel. And just like any other fire, if you don't put it out, your anger and hate will just go on forever.

Thirty years after my father sexually abused me, I still

hated him. I thought that if I stopped hating him, then my message to the world was that what he did to me was ok. I thought that if I stopped being angry at him, then that meant I was somehow letting him off the hook. My father was never punished by the law or anyone else for what he did to me, so I thought that the only retribution, the only resolution, the only justice I had was to hate him. If I never went to therapy, and I instead decided to take revenge on my father by hurting or killing him for what he did, like a movie hero, I still would have hated him after that. Killing him does not solve the problem that caused the emotion.

Without conscious awareness, anger and hate never end, and holding onto those feelings effects ME, not him. I could sit at home and hate him all day long and he would never know about it or be effected by it. Anger brings you down and disempowers you. It is the opposite of happiness. Hating my father never did me any good, and it didn't do anyone else any good. When you spell it out like that, anger and hate are pretty worthless.

As I moved through my personal journey of recovery, I realized that all of my hate was just keeping me from healing. Even though I realized this, however, I still needed to figure out a way to let go if it. I was looking in all directions for help and, finally, something brought my attention to meditation. I never saw myself as a person who meditates, but I saw images of people sitting very peacefully for long periods of time and thought how awesome that must be. I was so frustrated in my own skin, being angry and hateful all day, that I was willing to try anything new.

Using some simple instructions from a book on Buddhism, I found that simply sitting and breathing for just a couple minutes at a time was incredibly therapeutic. It brought the intensity of my anger down and, when I got up from my 2 minute "sitting and breathing break", I realized that I couldn't remember the last time I felt that peaceful. I was instantly sold on the power of meditation and began to take 2-minute breathing breaks at home, on my break at work and even sitting at a red light in my car. It was free and it was easy.

I started listening to simple guided meditations online that were 5 or 10 minutes long. These soon became too short for me and, before I knew it, I was sitting on my new meditation cushion, burning incense, and meditating for a couple hours a day. At the same time, I began to read books on Buddhism to see what else meditation could do for me and what other kinds of meditations existed. As I became drawn into Buddhism's simple, pleasant lifestyle practices, I very quickly became a calmer, happier person, moving through my day smoothly and finding a way to smile again at simply being alive. This was an enormous switch from the heavy emotions I had been feeling for so long and I started calling myself a Buddhist.

It's very important to understand that meditation wasn't a cure or a final solution. It's an empowering practice that calmed my anger and allowed me to see my situation clearly. On our individual journeys of recovery, when we find something that makes us feel a little bit better, it's very easy to decide to stay there. The peace and focus I discovered through meditation was not my ultimate destination, it was (and still is) a tool to curb the sometimes wild emotions and thoughts so that I could see more clearly and choose my next steps.

Recovery is a river that is continually flowing forward. It's important to have enough presence and awareness to notice when you're getting stuck in an eddy. It can be a nice place to pause, but it eventually gets stagnant if you stay there. On my continuing journey, I kept trying different types of meditation, reading books and even going to local meditation groups to explore how I could grow through this new, peaceful world I had found. I would soon discover a simple and powerful Buddhist meditation that would completely change my perspective of hate and anger forever.

DEPRESSION

Depression is one of the major symptoms people talk about regarding trauma. I listed it last in this chapter because depression to me is actually a side effect to a side effect. What I mean by that is there are direct effects of the abuse, like low self esteem, addictive behavior or anger. It was the inability to resolve these side effects of the abuse that seemed to cause my depression. When I could not figure out how to improve my self worth, how to stop my drinking, or how to change any of these other behaviors, I became depressed.

My doctors and therapists were quick to prescribe medication to mask the depression that I was feeling. Luckily, I never took them up on those offers. I think it can easily be argued that the reason depression is one of the most talked-about symptoms of trauma (mostly by the media) is because there are plentiful antidepressants on the market. Western medicine's focus seems to be to mask the symptom instead of eliminating the cause of the symptom. I instead decided to find out WHY I was depressed and to work toward eliminating the source of the depression. I'm so glad that I opted for self-improvement rather than feeding the pharmaceutical industry. I have known many people on antidepressants throughout my life and it always seemed to me like they were moving through their lives unconsciously and not actively healing. It was my awareness of the cause of my absolutely debilitating depression that allowed me discover the source and to let go of those behaviors.

Always look at the symptoms that you are feeling as signals from the body that there are underlying causes for those symptoms. Shine a light on these causes and work towards fixing them at the source. That is how I always moved ahead in my journey of recovery.

CHAPTER 5

COMPOUNDING FACTORS

"I had nothing to offer anybody,
except my own confusion."

- Jack Kerouac

WHAT ARE COMPOUNDING FACTORS?

I include this chapter because it was so important for me to realize that the pain I was feeling as an adult was not solely caused by the sexual abuse I endured as a child from my father. My world growing up was not just me and my abuser. There was a complex environment with countless points of influence that effected my emotions. There were many players in the drama of my youth who helped to shape my perspectives. Taking the time to unpack the entire panorama of my childhood environment and sort out the causes of my current pain points was a powerful step in my healing process. Once I identified the many different and sometimes surprising causes of my anger, submissiveness and other negative emotions and behaviors, I could release them, allowing me to move forward without them. Hopefully through listing the compounding factors that made up the totality of my abuse situation, you can better identify your own compounding factors in your life.

BYSTANDERS

My father and I were alone during the times I was abused, he made sure of that, but we did not live in an unpopulated world. We were surrounded by family, friends, teachers, coaches, neighbors, other adults and children. My father did not abuse me with nobody around to notice. He had to do it under the noses of many people who were around us almost all the time. Ultimately, these people either did not notice what was going on, or they did know he was abusing his children and simply allowed it to happen.

Realizing that the actual sexual abuse lasted for 9 years, and that my next older brother was most likely abused before me, possibly for the same amount of time or longer, it's probable that my pedophile father was abusing his children for eleven or more years without anyone noticing. The environment surrounding us at that time obviously made it possible for that to happen. Maybe not intentionally or consciously, but it certainly didn't keep it from happening. Let me say right here that I am not blaming the environment or the people around me at that time for the abuse my father inflicted on me. This isn't about blame, it's about clearly seeing the abusive environment of my youth. My point is that my complex web of interconnected emotions from this time in my life comes not only from my father's abuse, but also from how I felt about all of these other players in the drama of my childhood.

Aside from my father who abused me, my mother was next on the list of people who most influenced me during my childhood. I am not yet a parent, but I believe one of the most important responsibilities for a parent is to protect their children from harm. For years, I held onto a lot of subconscious anger towards my mother for not coming to my rescue when I was being abused by my father. I don't know if my mother knew that my father was abusing me, as I've never spoken to her about it, but I can see only three options. Either she knew it was happening and allowed it to happen, or she had some kind of feeling that something might be going on and ignored it, or she didn't know it was happening at all. If it was one of the first two options, clearly she should have done something about it. If it was the third option, that means she was completely oblivious that her husband was continuously sexually abusing two of her children for over a decade. In any of these scenarios, I was unconsciously angry because I felt that my mother failed in her duty to protect her children from harm. Whether she deserved it or not, I held onto that anger on a deep level for many years.

As a child, I didn't only exist in my house. I attended a six public schools, in 3 states and two countries, where I was surrounded by dozens of teachers and guidance counselors for 12 years. All through my school years, I made decisions and acted from a damaged emotional state. I repeatedly caused problems in class and got into a lot of trouble. None of my teachers or counselors ever responded by investigating what might be causing this behavior or what might be going on at home. Clearly none of them thought it was their job to do so. Again, I'm not blaming them. I'm looking at the environment I was raised in to identify the source of the anger that I have been carrying around my whole life.

Considering all the other adults in my life, like my piano teacher, my coaches, my friends' parents and others, I was holding onto a mountain of unconscious anger for almost everyone in my past. I had to deal with these feelings toward these other people with as much energy as I had to deal with the feelings toward my father, maybe even more so because there were so many of them. Not only is holding onto this much anger exhausting, this constitutes an enormous amount of emotional unpacking and examination to be able to identify this anger and let it go. I put a lot of energy into examining these feelings and sorting through them over the course of several years. This process allowed me to systematically let these destructive feelings go and eventually come to a place of peace with the people from my childhood world.

YOUR ABUSER'S RELATIONSHIP

If the person who abused you was in a romantic relationship or a marriage, then their relationship was clearly not an honest one. In a word, my parents' relationship was bad. This was absolutely a big part of the environment in which I was raised, and in which I was abused. I would go to sleep listening to them argue at night behind closed doors. Sometimes my father would put his fist into a wall or a door as they screamed at each other. I would find the damage the next day. My father was about 6 feet tall and over 200 pounds. I don't know if he ever got physically abusive with my mother when they were arguing, but the holes in the walls made it clear he was violently frustrated with himself and with their relationship. I don't clearly remember ever seeing them hug or kiss or have any kind of honest fun together. I mostly remember disagreements in public and arguments in private. I often wonder why they ever got married.

Like any child, I learned from my parents' examples. I saw my parents pretend to be a happy couple in public and then come home to be very angry with each other. So I learned from them that being two-faced is normal. Whenever I would visit my friends' houses and see their parents interacting in a happy way, my assumption was that they would fight at night, behind closed doors, just like mine did. These are definitely perspectives that I carried with me into my adolescent and adult relationships as well. When I started to get into my own relationships growing up, I would act a certain way with my girlfriends in public and then act differently when we were alone. I'm sure the women I was in relationships with were confused and most likely hurt by my behavior.

If your abuser was in a relationship, take a look back at it, if you are able. If your abuser was not one of your parents, like mine was, was your abuser married? Was he/she divorced or separated? Did your abuser have a relationship with someone who you knew or were friends with? Did you and your abuser have mutual friends who would not ever believe that he/she would abuse you? Or did they know about the abuse and do nothing? Were there other people around you who you feel, even subconsciously, could have prevented you from being abused or possibly have saved you after the abuse began? All these are good questions to ask yourself to determine what kind of emotional connections you had (or still have) to those people who were outside of the abuse situation but who were still within the world in which the abuse happened. Knowing where the anger or resentment specifically comes from, and who it is directed toward, will help you to identify it and let it go.

In retrospect, I think one of my grade school teachers was also a pedophile. He was an intimidating man, over 6 feet tall, broad-shouldered and short-tempered. He liked to physically handle the boys in our class and exhibited many of the warning signs of a child molestor I have since come to recognize. I knew he was married but, as a fourth-grader in his class, I didn't know anything about their relationship. I have heard, in recent years, that he left his wife because he realized that he was gay. If this is true, and if my suspicions about him being a pedophile were true, then he also came from a dishonest relationship. Living in a relationship that is not in alignment with your gender preference is definitely being dishonest with yourself, as well as the person you're in a relationship with. If his unhappy relationship led him to seek sexual fulfillment outside of his relationship, this could have been why he handled the boys in his grade school class so roughly, and why I have memories of thinking he was a pedophile. No matter what the truth is about him, I now realize that I had to deal with fear regarding this big man who was in my life so prominently at the time of my abuse. Looking back at this relationship, and identifying how it related to my own abuse situation has allowed me to release it.

THE CHEATER

When I was in grade school, I found out that my father was cheating on my mother with another woman. I knew this as a child and so did the rest of my immediate family, including my mother. She protested, but she lived with it. My father's mistress worked at his office. My father would tell my mother that he had to go into work after hours and, although we never talked about it, we all knew what was going on. As was the way in my family, there was no discussion or communication about this topic, so I was left to attach meaning to this on my own. He was setting a powerful example for me, leaving regularly to spend time with another woman instead of his wife and family. This fed my feelings of low self worth and helped define the word "love" as being superficial and meaningless.

I was mercifully distracted from my home life during this time by being a athlete. I was a member of a competitive gymnastics team growing up, which gave me a place to get away. We would meet for practice on a rigorous schedule; up to 5 times a week, 3 or more hours a night. My father would take these opportunities to drop me off at practice, go see his girlfriend for a few hours and then come back later to pick me up. He was often late and I would be left waiting outside the gymnasium for him at night after everyone else had gone home. Even though I was young, I knew what was going on. He would come back smelling like bad perfume and cigarette smoke. I felt unimportant to him. On the way home, he would talk to me with vaguely encouraging words about gymnastics and other things in my life, but this was only a surface-level interest. Even at that age, I could tell. He wasn't involved in my life in a caring way. All of his behavior reinforced that I meant very little to him. On my gymnastics nights, I was just an excuse for him to see his mistress.

My mother caught my father cheating on her after just a few months of infidelity. If my father could not maintain an extra-marital affair without my mother noticing so quickly, it just goes to reason that he could not have sexually abused two of his children for over a decade without her noticing either. A valid question for me to ask is that, if my mother allowed my father's affair to go on, could she possibly have known, or at least suspected, about my abuse and allowed that to go on as well?

This extra-marital affair had nothing to do directly with the sexual abuse he was inflicting on me, but it was part of an environment he created which continually taught me how little I meant to him. It also helped me put the pieces together of how complex my emotions were at the time. The enormous web of emotional connections between all these events in my early life was complex and challenging to disassemble, but taking the time to do it allowed me to see it all clearly and heal from it.

LEAVING

My father finally walked out on our family when I was in my early teens. Compared to the actual sexual abuse I endured, this event had a different but equally devastating effect on my personality as a child.

When I was 14 years old, I came home from school one afternoon to find my father loading suitcases into his car. My mother was at work, so it was just him and me at home. He told me that, when my mother gets home from work, I should tell her that he had moved out and wasn't coming back. Then he walked out of the house and drove away. So on top of everything else he had done to me, he dumped that responsibility onto me as well; the duty to inform my mother that he had left us. At that moment, in addition to everything else I was blaming myself for, I absolutely felt like it was me who made him leave - especially since he was making me tell my mother, which felt like some kind of punishment.

When my mother got home and asked me where my father was, I told her exactly what he told me to tell her. She exploded with anger and questions, as if there was more information that I was not telling her. She had no sympathy for the terribly unfair position my father put me in that day. She simply yelled at me. This exacerbated my already existing guilt regarding his leaving.

The afternoon actually got worse for me after that. The news I gave my mother was too much for her. After a few minutes of yelling, her blood pressure shot up and she suddenly fell over right in front of me. She hit the floor face down in the middle of the kitchen and laid there motionless. I was terrified and confused. I made sure she was breathing, then ran to the neighbor's house for help. When I got back, she was standing on wobbly legs, swaying back and forth and bleeding from her head and nose. It was an image out of a horror movie. I got her to lay down on the couch and eventually her doctor actually came over to our house to make sure she was ok. The doctor gave me medications for her along with instructions on how to deal with what was to be her confused state of mind for the rest of the evening. From that point forward, my father was gone and it was me she depended on to be the man of the house. It was me who began to take care of her.

Ultimately, my parents made me the conduit through which they ended their relationship. It wasn't until I was in therapy 30 years later that I realized the impact this single day had on my psychological definition of myself. I subconsciously thought I ended my parents relationship and I carried that guilt and shame into my adult life.

The lesson here is that other events in your past, which may or may not have been connected to the actual abuse, could be causing and/or compounding psychological issues in your current life. As I tell the story of my entire abusive childhood situation, I can focus on the years of sexual abuse as the "worst thing" that happened, but it's also easy to see how a day like this one can have an equally devastating effect on a young man.

If you have additional events in your life that may be either related to your abuse, or completely unrelated to it, it pays to give them some attention. Focusing solely on your abuse can overshadow some of these other factors that may still be having an effect on you. Take time to unpack, identify and examine the events surrounding and following the time of your abuse and I guarantee you will see some kind of connection.

MY ABUSER'S OTHER CHILDREN

When my mother found out that my father's girlfriend was pregnant, the arguments increased, but she didn't leave him. When she found out that the woman was going to keep the baby, she protested, but she still didn't leave him. Finally, a couple years later, when my father got his girlfriend pregnant a second time, my mother was outraged. She threw things at him from across the room; heavy things that broke other things, but she still didn't leave him. As a child, I watched all of this transpire. In addition to the example my father was setting with his lying and cheating, my mother was setting her own examples for me. She taught me that life is about taking abuse from the person you're in a relationship with. I had no role model in my life who was a fighter, who stood up to take care of themselves when being abused. I didn't learn how to stand up for myself until years later.

When I found out, along with the rest of my family, that my father had other children, I was deeply hurt and didn't know how to deal with those feelings. My own father was having children with a woman other than my mother and he was also spending time with them instead of us. He later left us to go live with them forever. Nobody was explaining to me that this was not my fault and I kept wondering what I had done to cause him to do this. Part of my young mind thought that I was such a bad child that he had to go have other children who were better than me.

I came to understand later, as an adult, that he was creating new children to sexually abuse and it had nothing to do with my behavior. I was simply getting too old for his sexual preference – what pedophiles refer to as their "age of attraction".

THE AFTERMATH

Having to deal with the aftermath of my parents' breakup was another ongoing contributing factor which complicated the already damaging side effects of the sexual abuse. My father was the breadwinner in our family so, when he left, he took the money with him. My mother and I were forced to move from our nice suburban home that my father had built for us, into a roach infested rent house across town. I went from being the wealthy kid, to being the poor kid overnight. My father took my college fund and my brother's college fund, that had been in our names since the day we were born, and used all that money to care for his new family. I took a job, working after school and on weekends, to help my mother pay rent and buy groceries.

Soon after he walked out, I had to go to court and watch my parents get divorced in front of lawyers and a judge. They made me decide who I wanted to live with. I chose my mother. I saw my father's girlfriend in the courtroom, sitting with her two children on her lap; my half-brother and half-sister. At one point, she caught me alone in the hallway of the courthouse and she took the opportunity to sit down across from me. She said, "I can't believe how badly you've treated your father." I silently got up and walked away. I never understood the logic behind that statement but, as a child, it reinforced my guilt, shame and low self esteem.

After the divorce, my father rarely if ever paid his alimony or child support and my mother and I were left to fend for ourselves. I left all of my extracurricular activities because we couldn't afford them. On the nights that I wasn't working, I would either go out causing trouble with my friends, or I would stay home to drink and smoke with my mother. She was depressed because of what had happened to her, and I was living in this state of subconscious shame that I had somehow caused it all. My mother had been married to my father for her entire adult life and was in shock to be living without him.

After my high school graduation, when it came time for me to move out and go to college, she was hurt again. I inevitably felt like I was the one hurting her. I did not see or place any value on my own needs in my life, only hers and what I was doing to her by leaving. All of these events, one after another, caused the mountain of unconscious guilt and shame I carried for our broken family.

Overall, the more I looked for compounding factors in my youth, the more I found. There was a lot to digest, but once I looked at these events and the actions of these people, I had the opportunity to take time and identify them. Once I shined a light on them and looked right at them, I was able to let them go, releasing their power over me. It will probably take the rest of my life to unpack, examine and identify absolutely everything I can remember, but I am already very far above the level of depression I was at only a few years ago, before I started this journey of recovery.

CHUCK TYLER

CHAPTER 6

REMEMBERING, ADMITTING
AND ACCEPTING

"For a seed to achieve its greatest expression, it must come completely undone. The shell cracks, its insides come out and everything changes. To someone who doesn't understand growth, it would look like complete destruction."

- Cynthia Occelli

HONESTY AND FEAR

I've talked a lot about honesty already and I'm going to reiterate it here. Just like working with a therapist, when you're working with yourself to remember what happened, to unpack and examine everything, it's not going to work unless you're totally honest. You have to be open and accepting with whatever you remember. Fear is a factor in being honest with yourself. If you're scared of what you're trying to remember, then you may be tempted to not be honest with yourself about it. Your mind will keep lying to you to keep you away from that thing you're scared of.

One of my therapists helped me to understand that, when I was a little boy being abused, the intense emotions I was being forced to deal with were unimaginably huge and scary to me, just as my father was so much bigger than me. At the time, my mind took these enormous emotions and locked them away in my mind with the memories. Now that I'm an adult and I am starting to access these memories, my mind still has them categorized as enormous, frightening monsters, because that's what they were to me when they were locked away. That little boy's fear-based perspectives are still in there along with all the memories. I looked at these memories and realized that the gigantic monsters of emotion were actually much more manageable to my adult brain. Once I realized this, it created a more comfortable perspective and I was able to unpack the past. I said to myself that I was able to handle it, and I did.

Whatever your abuse situation was, however long ago it happened and whatever your abuser did to you, it's important to realize that the emotions attached to that time in your life were bigger at that time than they will be when you unpack them now. Your fear of looking back at that time is based on the emotions you were feeling at that time. It's like a hot coal that you cannot hold because it will burn you. That coal has been locked away and has cooled off. You just don't know it until you unpack it and look at it. Be brave. Go find the truth. You will be rewarded by realizing these memories no longer have any power over you.

THE NAUSEA OF THE TRUTH

Even after going through therapy, talking to audiences and writing this book, I can still get nauseated when I think about what happened to me. It can even give me a physical feeling in my stomach that I'm going to vomit. Most of the time, I'm used to it and it does not cause that visceral reaction, but it does happen. Some people think that it's incorrect behavior if you don't get sick or disgusted when you talk about childhood sexual abuse. One important note is that this nausea is an ongoing indicator that I am not a person who would sexually abuse a child simply because that's what my father did to me. In this respect, the nausea is a good thing.

The more I thought about what happened to me, the more I realized how complex it was. Each layer that I would explore was another level of nausea for me to endure, but that didn't stop me. I was not going to let nausea get in the way of my healing and taking control of my life. Besides, the more I looked at my past, the more desensitized I became to the nauseating situations that kept revealing themselves to me. So I kept looking at everything I found, I used my presence - awareness - honesty model, and I kept digging deeper.

The first layer was accepting that I was sexually abused by an adult, and it started when I was 3 years old. This is a pretty terrible starting point. The next level was that my abuser was my own father, which added the word incest to the situation. The next layer is that we were both males, which made the abuse homosexual. I don't think the fact that the abuse was homosexual makes the situation worse than if it were heterosexual. It's fair to say, however, that because I have grown up to realize that I am a heterosexual adult, I find homosexual sex unappealing to engage in. That means that I had sex forced upon me that was not in alignment with my sexual orientation.

Also, because of my father's two-faced behavior, the homosexual element of my abuse exacerbated an already confusing situation for me. My father outwardly condemned homosexuals, even though he was in a sexual relationship with his own son. When I became an adult and started to examine this contradictory behavior, I realized how much of a mixed message this was giving me as I was growing up. Instead of trying to understand this at such an early age, my mind packed it all way for me to figure out later and hopefully heal from it. When the memories did begin to come back, it was still difficult to understand.

One of the most important things I have learned in my recovery is that I don't have to completely understand what happened to accept that it did, indeed, happen. I don't have to understand it to realize that it wasn't my fault, that it wasn't my choosing. And I don't have to understand it to realize that it's something that I, myself, would never do to children. Mostly, I did not need to understand what happened in order to let it go. "Understanding" is one of those concepts that can be a bottomless, black hole. You can try to understand something deeper and deeper and it can never end. I decided to accept what happened to me for what it was. If I came to deeply understand the events of my abuse during the course of my recovery, then great. But I did NOT need to dissect it to the point of driving myself crazy in order to let all that crap go. You can let it go without that deep understanding! I didn't let looking at my past consume me, I didn't let it scare me and I didn't let it control me — at least not to the point of backing away from it. I identified things, let them go and kept moving forward.

Whatever your sexual abuse situation was, do not be afraid to look it in the eye. Let yourself get nauseated, get sick and move past it. As someone once told me, if it growls at you, growl back. Whatever it was about that situation that made you the victim and made you powerless, all that has changed. You are now in charge. You have the power. You are looking at your past and deciding not to let it control you anymore.

TIME TO DIGEST

Recovery is not an overnight process. It takes time to change in a healthy way. It is important to take time to digest the information you are remembering, or that you are realizing about your abuse. After you let go of someone else's perspectives that you've been carrying around, and replace them with your own new ones, it takes time to practice applying those to your life and make them a part of your new, healthy behavior. Give yourself all the time you feel like you need, but do not use that time as an excuse to stop your journey of recovery.

Back when my first therapist helped me to realize that I had actually been abused, I decided to press the pause button on my therapy and take some time digest what I had learned. Realizing that I had been abused was a pretty big shock and taking that time was an important part of the beginning of my recovery. I was not, however, in a very supported environment back then when I found out this news. I had no friends or family supporting me and giving me outside eyes on what I was doing to help keep me on track. After I decided to pause my therapy, I told myself that I was taking time to digest what I had learned about myself, but eventually I began to ignore this new information and unconsciously began to work around it instead of through it. This turned into years of avoiding what I had just learned about my past.

I don't blame myself for doing this because my mind had already been hiding these memories for years. Hiding the memories was how I had survived up until that point, so it was a comfortable reaction for my brain to have. Instead of taking a short digestive reprieve from therapy, I found a major distraction that kept me away from my recovery journey for years.

I became involved with a woman who had also been sexually abused as a child. Her abuse went on for years, just like mine. She was as damaged as I was and she was ignoring the effects of her abuse instead of dealing with them. I saw her as a functional adult who had a career, a house and no apparent problems on the surface. She was open with me about not dealing with the abuse and I thought that if she was doing fine without dealing with her past, I should be fine without dealing with mine. I unconsciously thought that this relationship was a perfect match and I stayed with this woman for 9 years, never moving forward in my own healing process during that time. I got comfortable with ignoring what I had remembered.

I don't blame her for my stagnation. We are all on our own paths and we are all in different places in our journeys of recovery. My mind made a decision to regress on my journey instead of advancing. My mind thought I was strong enough to handle the truth about my past, but clearly I was not ready to deal with it. So, I ended up taking a step back. During this time, I took a job I hated, bought a house that was old and dirty, I drank alcohol and coffee at levels that probably should have killed me and I exhibited all kinds of negative, addictive and self-destructive behavior.

My advice is that if you take time away from whatever type of therapy you are involved with to give yourself the opportunity to digest information, make sure you don't get distracted or "comfortable" at the new level you've achieved. If you tell yourself that "you're better than you were before and that's good enough", then you're cheating yourself out of real forward motion and keeping yourself from the amazing life you deserve. You've already come this far, so you have proven to yourself that you have the ability to move forward. As so many people have said throughout history, that first step is the hardest. Just keep going. Go slower if you need to, take smaller steps, but keep going. See what's around that next corner, and the next one, and the next one. Just peek if you have to instead of charging forward, but keep moving. This way, you can create some momentum. I promise you that the empowering rewards of continuing your journey of recovery will be more than you ever thought they could be. They have been for me and I'm not done yet.

LOOKING AT "JUNK" MEMORIES

For those of us who are working to remember exactly what happened to us during our abuse, I have learned that absolutely everything I can remember about the time surrounding my abuse is important. I'm not talking about just the specific instances of abuse, but all the memories I can recover from that time in my life. Even if certain memories from that time seem unrelated, and you find that you could easily label them as "junk", don't arbitrarily ignore them. Take the time to consider them. Memories from my daily life, surrounding the time of my abuse, have helped me to put unexpected pieces together and ultimately realize a bigger, clearer picture of what was going on.

First let's take a look at what our minds typically choose to remember. Very few people have authentic photographic memories, but the vast majority of people don't remember their entire life from the time they were born to the current moment. What we actually have are pieces of an ongoing memory stream. We have selected bits of our lives that our minds chose to hold onto while it leaves the rest on the cutting room floor. I remember "big" things that happened to me, but not the little things. For instance, I remember when I had a motorcycle accident at 17 years old, which put me into a cast for months. But, I can't tell you what I was doing a couple days before that happened. So, if the brain only holds onto the times in our lives that made a big impression, then why do we have so many junk memories – memories of mundane moments that seem to mean nothing?

The conclusion I came to is that any memory that my brain is still holding onto must be worth looking at, whether it seems to be important on the surface, or not. I believe that even seemingly mundane memories that we still hold onto have value. I think they are a message from our minds that these seemingly unimportant memories should still be examined. It's telling us that there is a puzzle that hasn't been solved yet and these memories are the pieces. If they were totally meaningless, why would our minds be expending energy to hold onto them?

I took time to look not only at memories of my abuser's behavior, but the behavior of other people who were involved in my life at that time as well. Surprisingly, I found clues to my abuse in absolutely every one of these junk memories. All of them contained a thread for me to start pulling to help figure something out. It's as though my mind was holding onto these memories until I was strong enough and wise enough to put these clues together, then I could identify it, learn from it and heal. I don't think the brain makes mistakes. I don't think it holds onto memories meaninglessly. I think it wants to heal and it needs the conscious mind to do that.

For example, I remember sitting on the couch as a child watching TV with my family. It seems like a boring memory, but after I focused on it, I remember that my father came into the room, sat down on the couch and put his arm around me. I remember feeling so uncomfortable, that I got up and went somewhere else in the room. I don't remember what was on TV, what I was wearing, or what time of day it was, but I definitely remember what my father did and how I reacted. Clearly, this memory was a reminder of my father's physical invasion of my personal space and it stuck in my head as a clue. It was something I needed to remember so I could deal with it later. It was a thread to pull.

I remember standing at the front door of our house when I was very young. I was holding my fathers hand as he stood there talking to one of our neighbors. The man had his two children with him as well. The kids were a little younger than me and the 3 of us kids just stood there looking at each other while our respective fathers spoke to each other. This memory is still very vivid in my mind and it seemed to be meaningless for decades, but my brain still held onto it for me to ponder. I finally took some time and really tried to remember what happened that day. After some effort, I remember there was a momentary lull in the conversation and my father said, rather suddenly, "My god, you have beautiful children." The neighbor was quiet for a few moments, then awkwardly excused himself and walked away. Now that I took the time to remember it clearly, I can hear it to this day, over 40 years later.

I have many other memories of uncomfortable things that my father did in my presence. Any single one of them could easily be ignored as an awkward moment, but when I took some time to focus on them, the complete picture came back and I remembered more clues to my abuse. When I added them all up, it spelled out a behavior pattern. This process of examining junk memories was very valuable to me while I was working through all of my memories of what happened – and it still is to this day.

My advice is to welcome these random memories that you may have. Write them down if you have to, sketch out images if you like and look at them. Take your time and be as accurate as you can. Ask yourself, "why is my mind holding onto this seemingly meaningless memory from so long ago?". Ask yourself, "why would that person act that way in that situation?" Be honest with your answers, pull on those threads that your brain is holding onto and you may start to see patterns of behavior.

LETTING THE PAST DEFINE US

Looking at the past as something that happened to me long ago has been helpful to my recovery. What has NOT been helpful, in fact what has been a detriment to my recovery, has been spending most of my life using the past to DEFINE who I am today. It has taken me 40 years to realize the difference. This concept that "our past defines who we are today" is one of the biggest lies in all of humanity. It is right up there with "people don't change". Once I learned to let go of the belief hat our past defines who we are, I shifted into another gear and launched forward with my recovery.

Buddhist and Hindu beliefs teach us that we are born with personalities inside of us that are perfectly loving and full of compassion and peace. The environment we are typically exposed to as we grow up tends to cover up those personalities by burdening us with other people's belief systems. When we are taught to accept and see the world from other people's perspectives, we hold onto them as our own truths and, in doing so, we mask who we are underneath layers of other people's baggage. Our true selves are not gone, we are just covered up. We haven't been changed from who we truly are by adopting other people's perspectives, we have just been smothered. These belief systems that other people have given us, that we have accepted, are filters through which we see the world. They stain the decisions we make with other people's prejudices and dislikes. If we are present and aware enough to recognize these detrimental perspectives that we are carrying around, we can release them and let our true selves shine again. We're not "changing" who we are, we're uncovering who we are, rediscovering ourselves and allowing our true selves to come forward.

Anything that has happened to you in your past can be let go. Period. When abusers tell you who you are, when you learn a false definition of yourself through abuse, when something happens to you and hurts you or makes you confused, this is not a definition of who you are. It was not a definition of who you were then, and it does not define who you are today. All of this is a surface layer that does not belong to you. You can let it go and redefine yourself.

CHUCK TYLER

CHAPTER 7

FORGIVENESS AND LETTING GO

"One of the greatest gifts you can give yourself is to forgive.
Forgive everybody."

- Maya Angelou

WHAT IS FORGIVENESS?

There are so many words that I use in conversation every day that I have never looked up in the dictionary. I think most of us grow up hearing other people use words, then we extrapolate the meaning of these words through the way other people are using them. Then, we actually create our own definitions for them and use them in conversation based on these definitions that we've created. I grew up hearing the word "forgiveness" from many different sources. The one I remember most is when I went to Sunday school and to church as a child. I remember people repeatedly saying the phrase, "forgive and forget". Until I began to write this book, I had never looked up "forgiveness" in the dictionary.

My own definition of "forgiveness" had always included relieving someone of the responsibility for something bad they had done and somehow abandoning justice in the process. As a child, when my parents told me to forgive someone for some wrongdoing they had done to me, it meant that I had to go to them, face-to-face and tell them, "I forgive you". From my perspective, that person was then pardoned for their deeds and absolved of their responsibility. They no longer needed to feel guilty for what they did. Not only would they not be punished, but everyone was also supposed to forget about what they had done and move on.

After I began having memories of my abuse, and with this definition in my mind, I felt that I would never, ever, apply the word "forgive" to my father for what he did to me. I would never expend any of my energy to pardon him face-to-face for sexually abusing me when I was so young and powerless to stop him. With all the emotional trauma that I had gone through for so long, I would never intentionally absolve him of the responsibility or guilt for what he had done. I actually felt exactly the opposite. I wanted him to suffer like I had suffered my whole life. At the beginning of my recovery journey, I thought I could definitely work through whatever challenges I was having regarding the effects of the abuse without ever forgiving him as part of that process. I didn't realize how wrong I was.

Being someone who has now learned to pay close attention to the words I use when I communicate, I went to the internet and looked up the word "forgive". I found this definition:

"To stop feeling anger toward someone who has done something wrong. To stop blaming someone."

To my surprise, it didn't say anything about talking to the other person, or absolving them of guilt, or pardoning them without justice. It said to stop feeling anger, which is something I actually wanted to do. But it also said to stop blaming him, and that seemed impossible. If I was going to blame anyone for what happened, it was definitely going to be him. I was certainly at a point in my life where I was done blaming myself for what happened, and blaming him seemed obvious. This point in my recovery seemed like a brick wall; a dead end. I could not "forgive" my father because I felt like somebody had to take the blame for what happened. Somebody needed to remain unforgiven until they had "paid" for what they did to me.

MY JOURNEY THROUGH FORGIVENESS

After pounding my head against this brick wall for a while, I went looking for some guidance. I found myself shopping in the New Age section of a bookstore. Eastern philosophy had always appealed to me because I would see new age practitioners seeming to be at peace with everything, but I didn't really understand it. I definitely longed to be at peace with what happened to me. I was ready to start letting go of this blame that seemed to be holding me back from healing, but I had no idea how to go about it.

Many years ago, someone handed me a book called "The Power of Now" by Eckhart Tolle. I remember that I read the first couple of chapters, I thought it was ok, and I put it back on my bookshelf thinking I would give it to the thrift store. Somehow, I never did. Seven years later, I found that book in a box in my garage. I picked it back up and started reading it again. This time it shocked me. Eckhart's message was so clear and appropriate to what I was going through that it felt like a higher power was talking directly to me with every word. I read that book cover to cover, highlighting almost half of it and making notes in the margins. Then I bought his second book and quickly devoured it with the same excitement as the first. I was clearly ready to hear his message of healing and forgiveness. I wasn't ready to forgive my father yet, but I was absolutely beginning to look at forgiveness from a new perspective.

Next, I started reading other authors who's names would come up when I searched for Eckhart Tolle online. This chain of research ultimately led me to Buddhism. It seemed like Buddhism promised to make me at peace with everything. This is where I learned to meditate, which absolutely helped me, so I dove into Buddhism head first.

I learned quickly that there are many different kinds of Buddhism, some of which did not appeal to me at all. I wanted to start with the basics so I looked at Buddha's original writings and I applied something called "the eightfold path" to my daily life. This Eightfold Path explains how to think and act in every situation in life every day to achieve happiness. It's made up of:

- The right view
- The right intention

- The right speech

- The right action

- The right livelihood

- The right effort

- The right concentration

- The right mindfulness

Leaving all other aspects of Buddhism on the sidelines, I began applying the eightfold path to my life. It was actually a simple practice. Through this process, I started looking at forgiveness in yet a new light and I finally was ready to start creating a new definition for it.

The Buddhist practice of forgiveness focuses on looking at things clearly, accepting what you see and being honest with yourself. My new methodology became presence, awareness and honesty. This practice changed the way I looked at absolutely everything – including and especially my father and the way he treated me. I admitted to myself that I had made my father out to be a monster. Like so many other people who talk about pedophiles, I used the word "monster" repeatedly. But, through the practice of the eightfold path, I admitted to myself that my father was not literally a monster. He was a literally human being. Looking at him clearly, accepting that he was a human being and being honest with myself about this fact ultimately allowed me to take the next step and look at him in a new way.

My father sexually abused me, and that was really all I had been focusing on for decades. I now started looking at WHY he abused me. Instead of just saying that the was crazy, sick, demented or any other of a list of names I could call him, I really tried to attach a reason to why a person would sexually abuse their own children. I put myself into his shoes and thought what would possibly cause ME to sexually abuse my children. I could think of nothing that would make me do that. To this day, I have yet to discover his personal motivation. My father is no longer alive, so I can't ask him. I can only guess. But my methodology of presence, awareness and honesty led me to something I eventually realized was equally as important. It helped me discover what his motivation was NOT.

The earth-shaking turning point for me was realizing that he did NOT do what he did specifically to hurt me. This was a very difficult thing to admit to myself, but if I was being honest and looking at things clearly, it just made logical sense. If he wanted to simply hurt me, he could have beat me or tied me to a chair and tortured me. What he did do was perform sexual acts with me. His end goal was not to hurt me, it was to please himself. He was doing what he did to serve some emotional need in himself. In doing so, however, he was completely disregarding what effect it had on me. My damaged mental and emotional state was a side effect of him trying to fulfill some warped inner need that he had. He probably didn't even understand what that need was, but abusing his own children seemed to be the twisted solution in his mind, so he did it.

I came to the understanding that, as a human being, my father must have been going through something so challenging and confusing that he thought the only way to resolve it was to have sexual encounters with his children. I can't imagine what he could have been going through to come to that decision, but it must have been something incredibly confusing and emotionally devastating. He was not a monster, he was a human being; a very confused human being who made some unthinkably terrible decisions and hurt a lot of people in the process. But he was still a human being. I found myself saying that over and over again; my father was a human being.

The man needed help. He needed guidance. He

needed therapy. He needed someone to talk him out of trying to solve his inner turmoil by sexually abusing his own children. But that person did not exist in his world and he had no such guidance, so he became a child molester.

If a person has a drinking problem, that person could go to AA. If a person has anger issues, that person has the option of going into anger management therapy. If a person has a heroin addiction, that person could choose to go into a drug rehab clinic. In rural Oklahoma, in the 1970's, where does a pedophile turn for help? The small town we lived in was a racist, homophobic throwback to the 1950's. There was no place for him to turn for help. There were no systems in place to address the sexual urges of a pedophile and keep him from becoming a child molester.

Through this path of thinking, I had new questions to ask. Who do I really blame here? Do I blame my father for being mentally sick or misguided? Do I blame society for not being enlightened enough at the time of my abuse to have a facility to get this sick man some help? Or, do I blame nobody at all?

Blame, I came to realize, is just like anger and hate. It

goes on forever. When you label someone with blame for something they have done, that label sticks with them forever, if you let it. Blaming people gives you permission to be angry at them or to hate them. If you hold onto blame, you're holding onto anger and hate. So, instead of blaming him, I decided to look at the situation clearly, accept it for what it was and be honest with myself. That seemed to mean letting go of the blame and allowing it to change into some kind of understanding. Not approval for what he did, sexually molesting his youngest child for years, but the beginning of an understanding of why he did it.

Through this new perspective, along with hours of meditation, my anger for him slowly transformed into something surprising: pity. At first, it was an angry kind of pity. I found myself saying things like, "Wow, it must have sucked to be you, you sick, child-molesting asshole." But it eventually, slowly, surprisingly grew into actual sorrow for him. This new perspective on my father was such a big shift that everything in my life changed because of it. I looked at everybody differently. As I accepted this new view of my father, my thinking became clearer and my emotional state became more level and less frantic. The releasing of this blame, this hate and this anger for my father happened through a new definition of forgiveness. Looking at forgiveness as an internal release of anger and blame was a definition I was very happy with. It shifted my boiling anger for him into, not approval of what he did, but into a realization that he was sick and then into pity.

One of the biggest perspectives I learned though all my research was that each of us is doing the best we can in every situation, given our current state of consciousness. With my new definition of forgiveness, I could actually take anyone who had ever done wrong to another person, apply this new perspective to them and their situation, and come to the beginnings of an understanding of why that person did what they did. I wouldn't have to agree with what they did, condone it or justify it. I could still think it was absolutely wrong, but I would understand their motivation for doing it and not hold hate or anger for them. That person thought they were doing the only thing they could to resolve whatever challenge they were going through at the time. If they hurt someone in the process, if they shattered someone's life and gave them a lifetime of trauma, then it was clearly the wrong decision, but they must have been acting out of desperation. That's a point of desperation that I don't personally understand, but it only makes logical sense. Odds are that they didn't have the ability, resources or support to make a decision that could heal them or solve their problem. Instead, they resorted to hurting someone else or themselves. That person needed help, guidance, advice or counseling that they didn't get for whatever reason.

THE DEATH OF MY ABUSER

During the early stages of the creation of this book, I received a phone call from my brother. I was driving at night with my wife and she put the call on speakerphone. My brother said he just heard that my father had passed away two weeks earlier. My initial feeling was surprisingly non-emotional. It felt like I had just heard that someone who I did not know had died. After a pause, my first reaction was to say, "Ok... did he leave us anything?" I didn't feel loss, sadness or regret that I never spoke to him again. I just realized that he was not alive anymore.

Later, I had a realization — actually it was more of a visualization. I pictured myself standing in a kind of

211

bubble. This bubble was made up of all of the effects of the abuse that I was dealing with. Then I saw my father standing a long way away. He had no bubble around him and he was very separate and distant from me. I saw the image of him, way over there, and of me, encircled with the effects of the abuse. For the first time in my life, I became aware of a the very obvious physical separation between my father and the problems around me that I was dealing with.

From the time he divorced my mother, until the day he died, he physically lived several states away from me. Although he was alive, he wasn't anywhere near me and yet I was still traumatized by what he did to me decades before. At the moment of realizing his death, I finally wrapped my head around it. At that moment, I realized he may as well have been dead for decades because I never saw him, spoke to him, or was anywhere near him. Alive or dead, I was still carrying around the effects of the abuse he inflicted on me as a child. This really reinforced the importance of letting these heavy side effects go. This vision, at the moment I heard of my father's death, gave birth to a new perspective in me.

The pain and confusion I felt as a child, as I was going through the abuse, was absolutely and completely my father's responsibility.   But now, as an adult, it was completely my responsibility to do something with it. What I unconsciously decided to do, so long ago, was to keep that pain, to keep those perspectives he taught me and carry them around with me for 40 years.   It took me a long time to look at what happened to me as a child, from an adult perspective.   It took me a long time to use my status and strength as an adult to decide to let those things go.

I have now done it.   I have successfully let those poisonous perspectives go.   They are not a part of me anymore.   I'm a confident man who values and loves myself.   What it took me so long to realize was that it made no difference if he was alive or dead.   It was my decision all along to either hold onto, or let go of, all of the effects and perspectives that I was carrying with me.

TRANSITIONING INTO GROWTH

After these pivotal realizations, I felt like I was beginning to expand at an accelerated rate.   I could feel myself getting stronger.   The "me" that existed before the abuse was now coming forward. I had shed the weight of the side effects of the abuse, I had let go of the perspectives I had been taught and I was now finally being allowed to grow. Through these realizations, I felt like a new, strong foundation had been laid and I was building upon it. A wonderful and surprising side effect of this growth was that I was shedding fear. I simply stopped being scared of things. Was the fact that I was no longer scared of my father the reason or the catalyst for this new lack of fear? Probably. I now see absolutely everything I do as a fun adventure instead of something to worry about. I began to look at everything in my life from my own perspective instead of from a perspective that someone else had given to me. I was tearing apart my old, heavy paradigms and belief systems and wanting to redefine everything from my own perspective. The first thing I wanted to redefine for myself was love.

CHAPTER 8

REDISCOVERING LOVE

"You,

as much as anyone in the universe,

deserve your love and respect."

- Buddha

WHAT IS LOVE?

Like so many other words I learned as I was growing up, love is a word that was defined for me by my parents. As I pulled apart the events of my youth and examined them, it was clear that I needed a better definition than the one they gave me. Love is one of those words which means something different to everyone. Like the word God, love is probably one of the most historically misused and abused words in the English language.

My first definition of love was given to me before I could read. I was taught this definition by the verbal communication and actions of my parents. My father would tell me that he loved me and then he would sexually abuse me. I remember him saying "I love you" with an exasperated tone to his voice as though it were a consolation or even an apology. My mother would tell me that she loved me and then, for the most part, ignore me. When she said the words, "I love you" it was in passing as if to say, "see you later" or "pass the ketchup". My parents may have also given me an actual verbal definition of love when I was young, but I don't remember what it was. If their verbal definition differed from the way that they treated me, then I was taught that lies and broken trust were also a part of the definition of love.

Somewhere along the line, in those early years, I must have also learned from other people, from TV, or from being in the environment of grade school that parents were supposed to love their children. I'm sure that we were taught that we, as children, were supposed to be able to rely on our parents to protect us, teach us and care for our well-being. So whether I learned the actual definition of love from my parents or from my immediate environment, I surely compared it at some level to the way they were treating me and come up disappointed.

Merriam-Webster.com defines love as:

(1) A strong affection for another arising out of kinship or personal ties

(2) An attraction based on sexual desire

(3) Affection based on admiration, benevolence or common interests.

Interestingly, none of these definitions rule out the

possibility of a sexual relationship between a grown man and his young son. The word "benevolence" is in definition 3, but it seems to be used weakly, mixed in with "admiration" and "common interests". The word "affection" was prevalent in these definitions, so I looked that up as well and found this:

(1) A feeling of liking or caring for someone or something.

I was still unimpressed with this definition. "Liking" is also a weak and vague word, so I looked up "caring" and I found this:

(1) An effort made to do something correctly, safely and without causing damage.

Finally, a dictionary definition, two steps removed from the word love, that suggests "not causing damage" to the person that you have affection for. "Not causing damage" was clearly not part of the definition of love I was taught. In the early years of my life, even though I couldn't articulate it, I clearly associated love with disappointment, broken trust, abuse and neglect. That is not a positive start for a child learning about the world. Looking back on my early relationships, dating in high school and in my 20's, it's no wonder I acted in a self-centered way, or was uncaring of other's feelings. I used to beat myself up for how I acted in relationships as a young man but, being able to be aware and pay attention to the causes of those actions has allowed me to not only forgive myself, but to change that behavior.

If you had a relationship with your abuser that was supposed to be loving, as I had, think about how that person defined love through their abuse of you. Take some time to determine if that definition stayed with you after the abuse. If you adopted that person's definition of love as your own, even partially, it could explain some of the unhappiness you may have been experiencing in your life or your relationships since the abuse. Like other negative belief systems that you may have picked up and have been carrying around, let this one go and choose a definition of love that comes out of your heart rather than someone else's uncaring actions.

REDEFINING LOVE

Today, I don't use the word love lightly. When I say it, I am extremely aware of what I am saying. When I say "I love you" to my wife, I will hold her hand or put my arms around her and look directly into her eyes when I say it. I know the impact of what I'm saying and I know exactly what I want it to mean when the words come out of my mouth. I know that the energy I radiate when I speak to her that way delivers the message that I consciously intend it to. I have several friends who I tell that I love them. I know what I mean when I say it to them and it feels different to me. I'm sure they can feel it when I honestly say it to them as well. I let my heart shine whenever I speak these days and I don't put on the masks that my parents taught me to wear. I'm bring myself fully with everyone I meet.

I have also discovered something that I have heard other people call "unconditional love". I was experimenting with different kinds of guided Buddhist meditations when I came across one called "The Buddhist

Loving Kindness Meditation". This meditation shifted my perspective of both love and hate forever. The practice starts out having you sit and think about a person you love strongly. This could be your spouse, a family member, or even your child. While thinking about this person, intentionally decide to feel love for them. This is easy because you probably feel love for them anyway every time you think of them.

Next, you think about a very good friend that you have. While thinking about them, imagine that you feel a powerful love for that person. This is only slightly challenging because you may not call what you feel for them "love", but you definitely have positive feelings for them, so it's not a great leap to feel actual love for them. Go ahead and sit there, feeling love for them and experience that sensation.

Next, you think about a casual acquaintance or maybe a work colleague. Once you have that person in mind, think about what it would feel like to have great love for them. This might be a little different because you don't really know them. This challenges the notion of being able to love someone that you don't really know, but go through the practice anyway. Take a few minutes with each of these people. Really sit with the awareness of feeling love for them.

Then call someone to mind you don't know at all, like a random cashier at a store that you saw today. When you think about having a powerful love for that person, it may feel foreign or strange. Practice giving love to that person anyway. After all, they are a human being and are doing the best they can just like you. You have no reason not to love them.

As you work your way through this meditation, you next choose a person that you really don't like, perhaps someone who annoys you. Practice feeling love for them. This is where the meditation starts to really challenge you. It may be downright awkward, but do it anyway. It's a surprising exercise and will actually make you feel good when you do it.

Now, choose someone you would say that you hate. Bring them to mind and, you guessed it, really think about loving them. Be honest and really try to give love to that person from your heart. When I first did this, it felt like I was putting food in my mouth that I wanted to spit out because it tasted terrible. After doing it, however, I really felt that this meditation softened my perspective of them. I even tried intentionally choosing someone that I "hated" who I was going to see the next day. When I eventually DID see the person I practiced "loving" in my meditation the night before, the negative feelings I had for that person had eased. I didn't feel so heavy being around them. I never told any of these people what I was doing, but I kept doing it and I really felt that this meditation took the negativity out of my daily interactions with people. It was like magic. It was like magic that I was creating myself.

The meditation isn't over at this point, it actually ends with one more visualization. You finally bring an image of yourself to mind, as though you're looking into a mirror. Look yourself right in the eyes and, after giving your love to so many other people, point that big loving heart at yourself. You are the person you know more than anyone else in existence. You know the good, the bad and the ugly about yourself. Practice a feeling of love for every little last bit of yourself. Shine that light into every dark corner of your mind and love everything you can see – and everything you can't see. No judgment, just love.

I really suggest trying the Buddhist Loving Kindness Meditation. You can find a link to a Loving Kindness Guided Meditation that I created by going to my website, www.ChuckTyler.com. When I first practiced it, it was almost unbelievable that I could change my behavior by just sitting and thinking for a few minutes. It's absolutely not something we're taught to do in the west as we are growing up. I suggest doing it once a day for a couple of weeks and then be honest with yourself about the changes you see in your behavior and your emotions. My guess is that you'll surprise yourself with how well you will do at this practice, and how wonderful it makes you feel.

CHAPTER 9

BUILDING THE NEW YOU

"And the day came when the risk to remain tight in a bud
was more painful than the risk it took to blossom."

- Anais Nin

BECOMING THE PERSON I
ALWAYS WANTED TO BE

When I grew into my mid-20's, I remember telling people that I had become the guy I always wanted to be, and I remember feeling proud of that. Looking back on that time, I realize that the standard I was going by was something I had created in my mind when I was in grade school. A grade school kid who is in the middle of ongoing sexual abuse by his father is probably not in the best mental state to create a standard of what a balanced adult acts like. The dramatic environment of my youth had taught me how to give my power away, to be weak, passive and not trust anybody or let them close to me. That was the foundation on which I built this ideal image of myself. Now that I was taking my own power back and creating the new me, I realized that it was time to redefine this mental image of "the guy I always wanted to be".

I began by letting go of this old image and starting completely fresh. I had already shed many of the belief systems on which I based my view of life because they were toxic hand-me-downs from people who didn't really care about my well-being. I decided to maintain the practice of presence/awareness/honesty that had taken me this far in my recovery. I thought I would just bring that practice into my everyday life and observe how I acted with people. Then I could change whatever I didn't like.

With a little practice, being aware of the way that I currently act in daily life is actually very easy to do. It's been a very simple habit to create for myself and I've even made a kind of game out of it. When interacting with others in public, I listen carefully how I speak to people and how I act toward them. I silently analyze the what is happening and then decide if what I have just said or done paints me as the kind of person I want to be or not. I've done this so much that I even catch myself before I start to respond with something that I would categorize as the "old me". I stop and alter what I'm about to say so it fits my new definition of who I am now. I'm sure people have caught me smiling and not known that, while I'm casually talking to them, I'm actually in a constant state of self-improvement.

Throughout my years of recovery, I've read several books that describe how to painstakingly change who you are into the person that you wish you were. I've heard many methodologies on the subject from therapists as well. Personally, I have found that the way to change into the person that you really want to be takes two steps. It's so simple that you're probably going to laugh.

First of all, when you find yourself in a situation where you have to make a decision, think about the person you want to be and decide what that person would do or say in that situation. The second step is to immediately act that way in that situation. Simply do or say that thing. Suddenly, you instantly become the person who you want to be. All it takes is presence and a little sense of adventure.

I decided to do this all day, every day. It has become my life and who I am. No matter who you are or what your personality is, this model will create growth in you and help you suddenly become the person you've always wanted to be. It's a path back to your original self, the self that was covered up by the abuse. And the best part is that it's fun to rediscover it.

REPLACING NEGATIVE BELIEF SYSTEMS

The negative belief systems that you have let go may try to sneak back in and try to control the decisions you make. If and when they try, you will now be able to notice them and keep them from controlling you or staining your perspectives on the world. Through years of using someone else's belief systems, you will notice that the decisions you've made in your life up until now may have created relationships that do not serve you or brought physical things into your life that don't fit the person you are evolving into. Let your emotional state be your guide to help you identify these. In your new state of awareness, you should quickly and easily be able to identify when you're emotions are down. You'll be able to notice when you're unhappy with something or someone. This is actually a good thing. This is you recognizing an opportunity to change something so that you are happy instead of unhappy.

Be completely honest with yourself and look at what it is that's making you unhappy. When you find it, get it out of your life. Is it something simple like a chair in your living room or a shirt hanging in your closet? Is it something bigger, like your job? Is it a person in your life? Is it a behavior that you're exhibiting? Whatever it is, replace it with something that feels right, that feeds your empowerment, or that makes you happy. As hard as you've worked to become the new you, don't allow anything or anyone into your life that brings you down. Fill your life with empowering things and truly loving people.

If you are holding onto some simple thing in your life that is making you unhappy, it's caused by an underlying belief system. That belief system is telling you that, to be happy, you have to hold onto that thing. Clearly, it's not correct because you can now see that thing is making you unhappy. Definitely let that thing go but also take the opportunity to recognize the belief system that's making you hold onto that thing. Let this be an opportunity for you to recognize and release the belief system as well.

This also goes for people. If you are in a friendship, a romantic relationship, or a business relationship with a person who makes you unhappy, take an honest look at that relationship. If you are unhappy because the person does not respect you, then my advice is to let that person go. As I have said before, I decided years ago that anyone who does not treat me with respect is not allowed access to me. I decided that I simply don't have time for them. The way I let them go is to use the method I just discussed in the last section. I think about what the new me would say to them, and then I say it. When I have done this in my life, literally everyone who didn't care about my well being simply bounced off of me and went their own way. I never heard from them again. The people who did care about me are still in my life. They noticed that I was evolving and they supported me in doing so.

The important element in this process, and what will help you moving forward, is taking the time to honestly notice why you were involved with these toxic people in the first place. If you are in a bad relationship, then you put yourself there. Ask yourself why you would get involved with someone who did not respect you. Ultimately, with very little digging, you'll discover a belief system that you're holding onto that allowed, or prompted, that relationship to happen. Use this logical process of elimination to find it.

Ask yourself what you would possibly have to believe to allow someone like that into your life. Maybe you thought that you weren't worthy of a friend who respects you. Maybe you thought you needed someone to make decisions for you because you were incapable of trusting your own decisions. Whatever the ugly or difficult-to-admit truth is, allow yourself to face it. You will know that you have found the toxic belief because, when you say it out loud, it will sound absurd. It will sound like someone else's belief system. It won't sound like you. At that point, now that you're aware of it, you can release it. Just let it go.

I find that I'm typically laughing when I release mine because I find it hard to believe that I've held onto it for so long. It feels like dropping someone else's baggage that I've been carrying around for years. I feel emotionally lighter.

This is the point that you get to create new belief systems for yourself. I usually replace the old ones that I'm releasing with new ones that are pretty much exactly the opposite of the old ones. If I discover a belief system operating in me that says I need someone else's approval for what I'm doing, I replace it with one that says that I decide what course of action is best for me, regardless of what other people think. If I find one that is telling me that I should dress a certain way because that's what I've always done, then I replace it with one that says I'm going to buy something I've never worn before. And if I like how it makes me feel, I'm going to keep doing it. If I find one that is telling me that I should stick to doing what I'm good at and never try anything new, then I replace it with one that says I will try something new whenever I get the chance, so I can discover what else I can become good at. Replacing old, acquired belief systems with your own new ones launches you toward your true self at light speed. And, again, it's so much fun.

SECRET WEAPONS FOR SELF-EMPOWERMENT

In addition to actively examining myself and making improvements, there are things that I choose to do every day which help to keep me strong and empowered. My favorite secret weapon for empowerment is to find something you can do that makes you feel strong and do it whenever you can. Make it something that you consciously decide to spend your time doing. Bring it into your life as a regular practice. I have several of these things. Here are a few suggestions.

Ride a motorcycle. If you don't know how, go learn. That's what I did. There is a state-sponsored motorcycle operator's safety training course in every state. You can walk into that weekend course without ever having laid a finger on a motorcycle and you'll walk out riding with confidence. The instructors even give you your driver's test at the end of the second day. Then go buy a motorcycle and ride it to work every day. There's nothing quite like riding a motorcycle. It's so much more fun and empowering than being inside of a car. It brings me present, makes me more aware of my surroundings and just makes me feel more alive.

Meditation was the first thing I did that made me feel powerful. I highly recommend it. I believe every human being on the planet should practice some form of meditation daily, even if it is only for a few minutes. For me it recreates my mind as the number one place to go for safety, which is the polar opposite of what my brain used to be for so many years. My mind used to be filled with hidden memories and things to avoid. Now it's the safest, most loving place I can go when things get stressful, overwhelming or if I need an answer to something that's been puzzling me. If you're avoiding meditation, honestly ask yourself what you're afraid you might find when you go inside yourself. You are the last person you should be afraid of. Get in there and start redecorating your home.

Yoga is another one of my favorite empowerment practices. It doesn't matter how old your are, what shape you are, or how athletic you are. Yoga is a practice of spending time with yourself. I started many years ago by going to a few classes. Then, I did some research and came up with my own routine that I practiced at home every morning. I did it in hotels when I was traveling on business and I even did it early in the mornings in a guest room when I was visiting friends out of town without them knowing. Not that I was trying to hide it, but it had nothing to do with them. It was something for me. It was mine. I did it because I love myself and it made me feel strong. Eventually, I took a 32-day immersion course and earned my Yoga Instructor Certification. From that experience, I quickly created a therapeutic Abuse Survivor's Yoga Workshop to help empower people through the practice of yoga. I now teach yoga and practice daily on my own at home.

If you're a more social person, or if you WANT to

be a more social person, I found something that completely surprised me as a fun, therapeutic practice. My wife talked me into going to a drop-in beginner improv comedy class when we were living in Denver. I was very nervous the first time I went but, now that I've been to different ones hosted by different organizations, I've found that the improv community is extremely supportive and loving to one another. If you don't consider yourself to be a comedian, know that improv is not about being funny. It is about working together, supporting each other, being present, being honest, building trust with others and spontaneously creating something together from your heart. It's truly one of the most amazing things I've found in my life. It's a creative playground for adults that always leaves me feeling proud of myself at the end of a drop-in class. I've carried the powerful communication and relationship skills I've learned from improv into my personal and professional life. It has made me infinitely more comfortable talking with strangers, it has made me a more present and aware friend and it has absolutely helped me become a more confident spontaneous public speaker as well.

Experiment with new things. Hiking, biking, knitting,

martial arts, painting, teaching, gardening, volunteering somewhere, or maybe even take a new job in something that just sounds interesting. If you find something that you don't like at all, then drop it. The act of trying something and deciding not to do it is you taking care of yourself by setting boundaries for yourself. When you find something that makes you feel empowered, then intentionally decide to spend regular time in your life doing it. Pretty soon, your life starts to fill up with things you're doing that empower you and you don't have any more time for those things that don't excite you. Every day becomes a new adventure in self-empowerment. When you do this, you're telling yourself that you love yourself. You're getting to know your true self, and you're aligning your intentions with it.

NEW FRIENDS

Keep your support system strong and expand it whenever you can. This is no longer a support system for your recovery from sexual violation, it's a support system for your life. Make new friends who care about you and accept you for who you are. Pick people who want to be around you, and who you want to be around. If either of those are faked, it's just not going to work. Let go of all the people who don't fit these criteria and don't look back.

You may experience old friends wanting to reconnect with you. As much as I have changed through the last several years of my life, I am open to old friends being able to change as well and fit my new criteria, but I don't try to change them. If any of your old friends or family want back into your new inner circle because they say they have changed, or because you think they may have changed, you may want to give them another chance. It's your decision. You are in charge. Be firm and do what's best for the new you. Think about what the person you always wanted to be would do, and then do that. Create your new boundaries and maintain them. You have designed and manifested this new self, and you love yourself, so don't give anyone access to you if they just want to try to tear you down.

If you do decide to let someone from your past back in, be carefully aware of how YOU are acting around them. I've found that even at my most heightened state of awareness, I can fall back into old, destructive behavior patterns within seconds of being around someone from my past. Family members are the most powerful forces that can pull you back into the old you. Your family knows the old you, knows all your old mistakes and behaviors, and can unconsciously "team-up" on you with their influence to try to discount the new, powerful you. Sometimes I catch when I'm falling prey to this influence and sometimes I don't. Go easy on yourself without judgment, but be strong.

Back when I was the old me, I would have what I used to consider to be a great time with some people. Spending time with them now elicits old behavior patterns very quickly that used to make me think I was happy, but which don't anymore. This can be confusing and deceiving. In these situations, people in your support system might be able to tell you what they think. My wife has pointed out behaviors in me that I have totally overlooked. It was only after she pointed them out that I was able to notice them. This is why we need to keep our support system alive and strong, so we can keep moving forward in a healthy way.

These days I take every opportunity to make new friends. I go to business mixers, networking events, and I accept people's invitations to gatherings where I don't know anybody. Communication with people is now a game of being my new self and seeing who bounces off of me and who sticks. When you're present and honest, you're radiating a higher frequency of energy. If you maintain that frequency when meeting new people, they will either have to raise themselves up to meet your higher frequency, or they will not be compatible and wander off. This new set of friends you make will be more honest and caring than any friends you have ever had.

HONESTY AND AWARENESS

Maintain the highest level of honesty with yourself at all times. Now that you have a new skill set of being aware and forthcoming with yourself, you'll notice immediately when you're lying to yourself. When you lie to yourself consciously and then you let it happen and live with it, you're treating your best friend, you, in the worst way. Don't waste your energy judging yourself. We're all human, which means we all find ourselves doing things that we don't want to do for one reason or another. When you notice that you're lying to yourself, take a moment to be happy. The fact that you're noticing what's happening is proof of how far you've come. Situations that will try to lure you into being the old you will never go away. This is just life offering you the option of going back to the way you were. Be the new you and politely refuse it as you laugh confidently. The more you decide to be the new you, the more you continuously prove how incredible you are for making it here and deciding to stay here. Your own self-honesty and awareness of what you're doing will take care of you for the rest of your life.

THE ONGOING ADVENTURE

Looking back on where I came from and comparing it to where I am today, I realize that I have finally become a conscious player in my own life. Through the abuse, and honestly because of the abuse, I am now a force of nature for my own self improvement. For years I was buried in the mud under a dirty, stagnant pond. Today, even though I'm still discovering and working through more effects of my abusive past, my head is not only above water, it's

WAY above water. In fact, I feel like I'm flying. I never thought feeling so happy and empowered was possible, but here I am.

Some therapists and self-help books say that recovery never ends and I partially agree with that. I've learned that recovery becomes something else. It evolves. It turns into a new practice which, if you consciously let it, becomes your new state of being. Recovery becomes ongoing reinvention, ongoing self-improvement and ongoing discovery of who you really are and what you can achieve. It's a flowing river that is continuously moving forward toward growth, expansion and more empowered states of being.

I don't know if I ever would have chosen this path of self-examination and self-improvement so vigorously if I had not been so terribly abused as a child. I don't know if I ever would have appreciated and valued my own power if it had not been so blatantly and violently taken away from me and if I had not had to work so hard to take it back. I am the strong, confident, ever-growing man I am today because of the ugly way my father treated me for years when I was a boy, and because of the environment that surrounded the abuse.

Not only do I no longer hate or blame my father for what he did, I'm at a stage in my own incredible growth that I almost want to thank him. That may sound unbelievable, but I love who I am today, and I am who I am because of what I have gone through to get here. Do mountain climbers take a moment to thank the incredibly tough climb up the side of the mountain when they've gotten to the top? Or do they talk about how difficult it was for the rest of their lives?

Never stop on your journey. You're never done growing, expanding and self-improving. Keep getting stronger, keep becoming healthier, keep learning how to love more deeply and more honestly. Discover who you were before you were stained by someone else's actions and before you were burdened by other people's toxic belief systems. Relax into being that person and allow your self-created perspectives to grow every day. Embrace the strength and discipline that you already have so you can grow beyond anything that you ever thought you could become. And, for your own sake and everyone else's, please share your story.

CHUCK TYLER

"So certain are you.

Always with you what cannot be done.

You must unlearn what you have learned.

Try not.

Do… or do not.

There is no try."

- Master Yoda

CHUCK TYLER

Index

ABOUT THE AUTHOR

Chuck grew up with his family in a small Oklahoma town. As a young
man, he was a competitive gymnast and martial artist. He spent three years
serving his country in the U.S. Army and earned a BA in Visual Arts.
During twenty seven years living in Colorado, he fell in love with
backpacking, skiing, the outdoors and his wife. He recently walked away
from his career in television video production and advertising
to find a quieter life with more personal meaning.
Chuck now lives in Sedona, Arizona, with his wife
where he speaks on sexual abuse,
is an avid hiker and teaches yoga.

www.ChuckTyler.com

20806524R00144

Made in the USA
San Bernardino, CA
07 January 2019